LONGMAN
SOCIAL STUDIES

LeeAnn Aguilar Lawlor
Julie Mariscal

Longman

Longman Social Studies

Pearson Education, 10 Bank Street, White Plains, NY 10606

Vice president, primary and secondary editorial: Ed Lamprich
Senior development editor: Virginia Bernard
Development editor: Deborah Maya Lazarus
Editorial coordinator: Johnnie Farmer
Editorial assistant: Emily Lippincott
Vice president, director of production and design: Rhea Banker
Associate managing editor: Jane Townsend
Vice president, marketing: Kate McLoughlin
Senior manufacturing buyer: Nancy Flaggman
Cover design: Rhea Banker
Text design and composition: Quarasan
Text font: 12.5/16 Minion Regular
Credits: See page 292.

We gratefully acknowledge the contribution of Delia Estrada.

Library of Congress Cataloging-In-Publication Data
Lawlor, LeeAnn.
    Longman social studies / contributors LeeAnn Lawlor, Julie Mariscal.
        p. cm.
    Includes index.
    ISBN 0-13-193025-7 (alk. paper)
    1. Social history. 2. Civilization. 3. World history. 4. United States—History.
        I. Mariscal, Julie. II. Title.
HN8.L377 2006
909—dc22

                                                           2005004754

LONGMAN ON THE **WEB**

Longman.com offers online resources for
teachers and students. Access our Companion
Websites, our online catalog, and our local
offices around the world.

Visit us at **longman.com**.

ISBN: 0-13-193025-7

Printed in the United States of America
2 3 4 5 6 7 8 9 10–QWD–09 08 07 06

Contents

Unit 2

The Classical World 64

Unit 3

The Middle Ages 98

Unit 4

The Renaissance 132

Unit 5 — Early United States 166

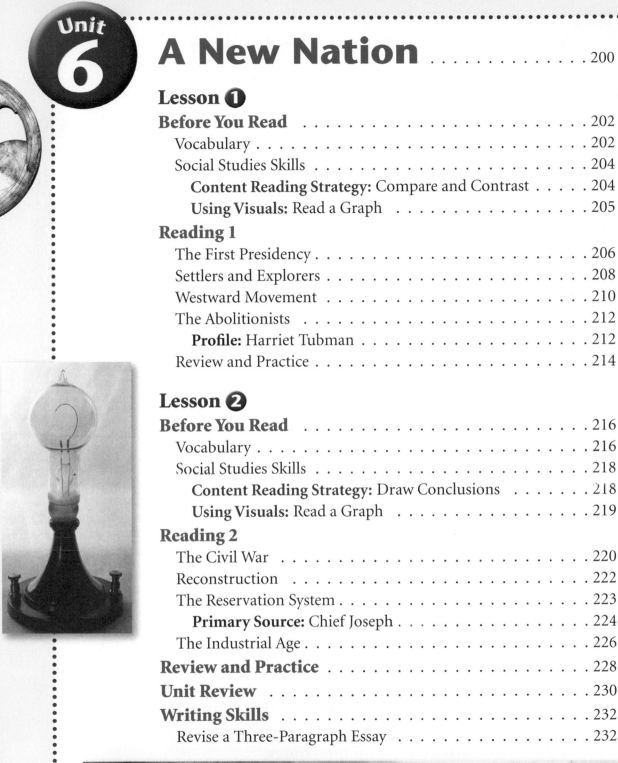

Unit 6

A New Nation 200

To the Student

Welcome to

LONGMAN
SOCIAL STUDIES

This book will help you learn about social studies. You will learn about world history. You will also learn about geography and how it relates to history. This book will help you be successful in your other social studies classes.

Before each reading, you will learn important words. These words will help you understand what you are reading. You will also learn how to use reading strategies and visuals such as maps and charts to help you understand the reading.

As you read, language tips will help you understand English grammar and vocabulary. You will also learn more about interesting people and events all over the world.

At the end of each unit, you will learn the process of writing. By the end of the book, you will know how to write a short essay.

We hope you enjoy *Longman Social Studies* as much as we enjoyed writing it for you!

LeeAnn Aguilar Lawlor
Julie Mariscal

Introduction

What Is Social Studies?

   We call history, geography, economics, and government *social studies*. When we study social studies we learn many things about a society.

   A society is a group of people who live in the same country and have the same customs. There are many ways to study a society.

▲ A crowded market in Bangalore, India

History

History is the study of things that happened in the past. History helps us understand people. We learn about the past and how it influences the present. We can learn facts about the people and places in the past. We can also learn about the present when we study the past.

▲ The ruins of the Museum of Science and Technology in Hiroshima, Japan. In August 1945, an atomic bomb destroyed the city. Today the ruins of the museum are a memorial.

Geography

Geography is the study of countries, oceans, mountains, and weather. You can learn about a place when you look at a map. Geography can influence history.

This satellite photo shows the Americas and the Pacific and Atlantic oceans. ▼

Economics

When you study economics, you study the ways that money, goods, and services are made and used. Goods are things like clothes or food. Services are things like schools and hospitals that people can use. When people buy and sell goods or services, we call this trade.

▲ People buy and sell goods at a market.

Government

The people who control what happens in a country are the government.
The government of the United States is democratic. *Democratic* means
that everyone has an equal right to vote and choose the leaders of the
government.

▲ People in a democracy elect their leaders.

**For more practice,
go to Workbook pages 1–3.**

The Five Themes of Geography

Learning about geography can be a huge task. The task can be easier if you study themes of geography. A theme is a main idea that can help you understand information. There are five themes of geography.

① Location

This theme answers the question, "Where is it?" *Location* tells you where an area is.

▲ Students locate a place on a map of Africa.

② Region

Regions are areas that share at least one common feature. For example, Thailand and Burma are both countries in Asia. They are both near the equator. They are both in the tropical region.

▲ Phi Phi Island, Thailand, is in a tropical region.

❸ Place

Every area has features that make it different from other areas. These features can be people, climate, landforms, or plants. We call this theme *place*. A place is a description of the physical and human characteristics of the area.

▲ Los Angeles is a place in California.

④ Movement

You can learn about the geography of the world when you study how people, things, and ideas move from one place to another place. This is called *movement*.

▲ Early settlers in the United States moved westward to look for gold and a new life.

❺ Interaction

The theme of *interaction* helps you understand how humans affect the world around us and how the world affects us. People often make changes to their environment to make their lives better.

▲ The Hoover Dam on the Colorado River provides electricity to the western United States.

For more practice, go to Workbook page 4.

Geographic Terms

There are many words you have to learn when you study geography. Look at the list below to see the words and their definitions.

Word	Definition
Bay	a part of an ocean that is enclosed by a curve in the land
Canyon	a deep valley with steep sides
Cliff	an area of high, steep rock, often close to the ocean or at the side of a mountain
Climate	a pattern of weather in a place over a long time
Coast	the land next to a sea or an ocean
Continent	one of the large areas on the earth (Africa, Antarctica, Asia, Australia, Europe, North America, South America)
Delta	a low area of land where a river separates into many smaller rivers flowing toward an ocean
Desert	a large area of land where it is hot and dry
Glacier	a very large area of ice that moves slowly over the ground
Gulf	an area of an ocean with land on three sides of it
Hemisphere	half of the earth
Hill	an area of high land; a small mountain
Island	a piece of land surrounded by water
Lake	a large area of water with land all around it
Mountain	a very high hill
Ocean	a very large area of salt water (Arctic Ocean, Atlantic Ocean, Indian Ocean, Pacific Ocean, Antarctic Ocean)
Peninsula	a piece of land with water on three sides
Plain	a large area of flat land
River	a continuous flow of water that goes into an ocean or a lake

Word	Definition
Sea	a large area of salt water that is smaller than an ocean
Valley	an area of lower land between rows of hills or mountains
Volcano	a mountain with a hole at the top that burning rock and fire can come out of
Weather	the temperature and the state of the wind, rain, and sun

Practice

Look for some of the words in the picture below.

For more practice,
go to Workbook pages 5–6.

Globes and Maps

The most common tools that we use to study geography are *globes* and *maps*. A map is a drawing of a city, a country, or the world. A globe is a ball with a map of the world on it. Globes and maps are used for different things.

Globes

A globe is about the same shape as the earth. It can show correct shapes. You can see how big or how small something is compared to something else. You can also see how far one thing is from another thing. A globe is harder to use than a map because everything on a globe is very small.

A globe ▶

Maps

A map is a flat drawing. It is easier to use than a globe because you can see more detail. Maps do not show the correct size and shape of every feature.

There are many different types of maps. Each type of map has a special purpose. You can get different types of information from different types of maps. As you study social studies, you will use many types of maps.

Mapmakers include features to help us understand the information on a map, for example a *compass rose*, a *scale*, and a *key*. Look at the map of Australia and New Zealand to learn about these features.

▼ A map

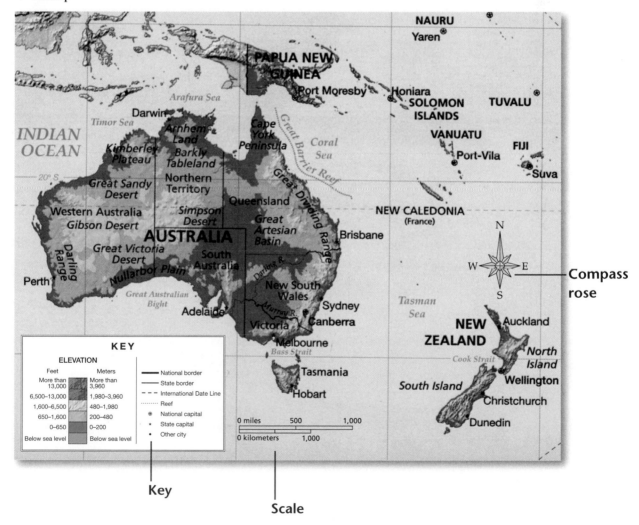

Compass rose

Key

Scale

Physical Maps

A *physical* map shows what an area looks like. It shows important physical features, such as hills, rivers, and plains. The key on a physical map often shows elevation, or the height of the land above the sea. Mapmakers use colors to show elevation.

Practice

Look at the physical map of Africa on page 17 and answer the questions in your notebook.

1. Name a desert in southern Africa.
2. Name a mountain range in northwest Africa.
3. What is the highest mountain in Africa?
4. Is this mountain higher than 13,000 feet?
5. Name the long river in northeast Africa.
6. Is the Atlantic Ocean east or west of Africa?
7. About how many miles apart are the Ahaggar Mountains and the Atlas Mountains?

Look at the physical map of the world on pages 18–19 and answer the questions in your notebook.

1. There are seven continents in the world. What are they?
2. Name the world's oceans.
3. What is the largest mountain range in North America?
4. Name a long river in South America.
5. What two continents have the highest mountains?
6. What is the elevation of these mountains?
7. About how many miles is Antarctica from Africa?

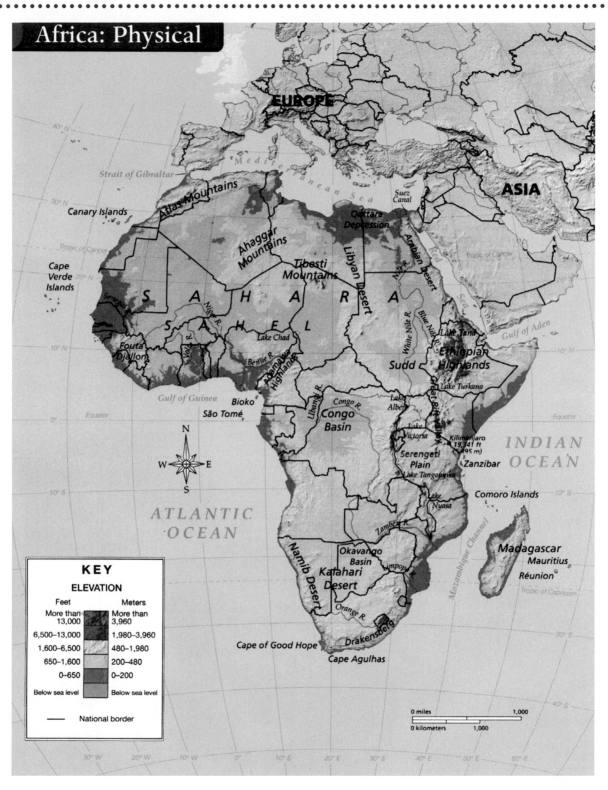

Africa: Physical

KEY

ELEVATION

Feet		Meters
More than 13,000		More than 3,960
6,500–13,000		1,980–3,960
1,600–6,500		480–1,980
650–1,600		200–480
0–650		0–200
Below sea level		Below sea level

—— National border

0 miles 1,000
0 kilometers 1,000

▲ A physical map of Africa

The World: Physical

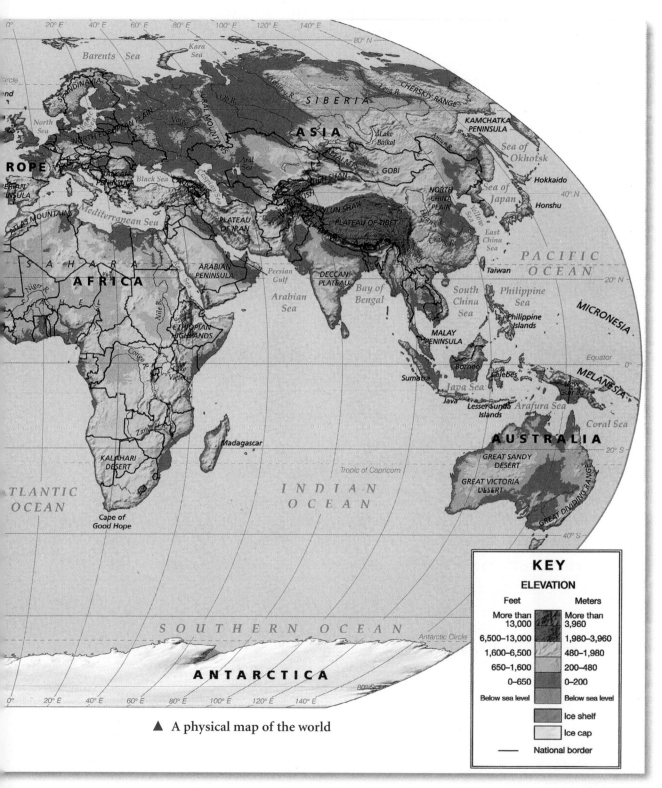

▲ A physical map of the world

KEY

ELEVATION

Feet		Meters
More than 13,000		More than 3,960
6,500–13,000		1,980–3,960
1,600–6,500		480–1,980
650–1,600		200–480
0–650		0–200
Below sea level		Below sea level
	Ice shelf	
	Ice cap	
—	National border	

Political Maps

A *political* map shows countries, states, or regions. The colors on a political map make the map easier to read. Political maps also show the names of towns, cities, and capitals, the main cities where each government is. Remember to look at the map title, scale, compass rose, and key to help you understand the map.

Practice

Look at the political map of Africa on page 21 and answer the questions in your notebook.

1. What countries are east and west of Libya?
2. What countries are north and south of Angola?
3. What is the capital of Morocco?
4. What countries share a border with Mali?
5. What direction is Egypt from South Africa?
6. What is the capital of Somalia?
7. Does Rwanda share a border with Uganda?

Look at the political map of the world on pages 22–23 and answer the questions in your notebook.

1. Name three countries in North America.
2. Name three countries in South America.
3. What direction is Russia from India?
4. What is the capital of Australia?
5. Does China share a border with Pakistan?
6. What country is south of the United States?
7. What is the capital of Chile?

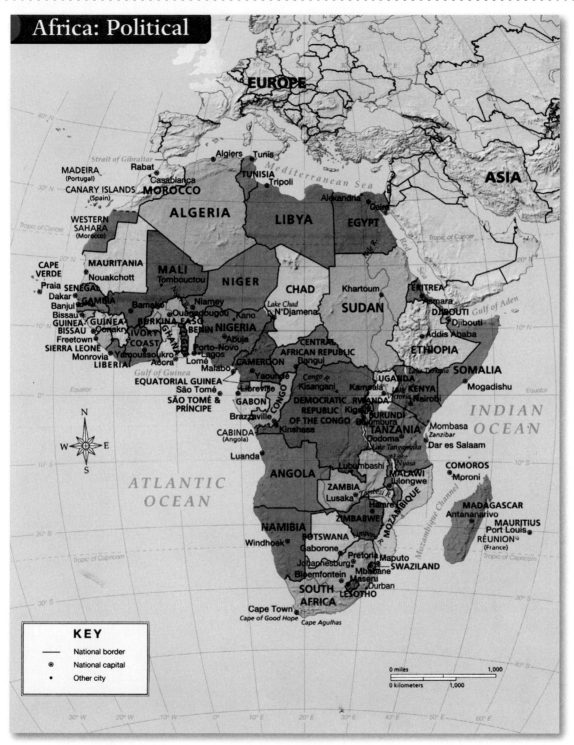

Africa: Political

EUROPE

ASIA

Strait of Gibraltar
MADEIRA
(Portugal)
CANARY ISLANDS
(Spain)
Algiers   Tunis
Rabat
Casablanca
TUNISIA
Tripoli
Mediterranean Sea

Alexandria
Cairo

WESTERN
SAHARA
(Morocco)
MOROCCO
ALGERIA
LIBYA
EGYPT
Tropic of Cancer
Nile R.
Red Sea
Tropic of Cancer

CAPE
VERDE
Praia
MAURITANIA
Nouakchott
MALI
Tombouctou
NIGER
CHAD
Khartoum
ERITREA
Asmara
DJIBOUTI
Gulf of Aden

SENEGAL
Dakar
Banjul
GAMBIA
Bamako
Niamey
Ouagadougou
Kano
Lake Chad
N'Djamena
SUDAN
Djibouti
Addis Ababa
Bissau
GUINEA
BISSAU
GUINEA
Conakry
Freetown
SIERRA LEONE
Monrovia
LIBERIA
IVORY
COAST
BURKINA FASO
BENIN
GHANA
Yamoussoukro
Accra
Lomé
NIGERIA
Abuja
Porto-Novo
Lagos
CENTRAL
AFRICAN REPUBLIC
Bangui
ETHIOPIA
SOMALIA
Mogadishu
Equator

EQUATORIAL GUINEA
São Tomé
SÃO TOMÉ &
PRÍNCIPE
Malabo
Yaoundé
CAMEROON
Libreville
GABON
Brazzaville
Congo R.
CONGO
Kinshasa
CABINDA
(Angola)
DEMOCRATIC
REPUBLIC
OF THE CONGO
Kisangani
Kampala
UGANDA
RWANDA
Kigali
BURUNDI
Bujumbura
Lake Victoria
KENYA
Nairobi
Lake Turkana
Lake Tanganyika
TANZANIA
Dodoma
Mombasa
Zanzibar
Dar es Salaam
INDIAN
OCEAN
Equator

Luanda
Lubumbashi
Lake Nyasa
COMOROS
Moroni
ATLANTIC
OCEAN
ANGOLA
ZAMBIA
Lusaka
Zambezi R.
MALAWI
Lilongwe
MOZAMBIQUE
Harare
ZIMBABWE
Mozambique Channel
MADAGASCAR
Antananarivo
MAURITIUS
Port Louis
RÉUNION
(France)

NAMIBIA
Windhoek
BOTSWANA
Gaborone
Limpopo R.
Pretoria
Johannesburg
Maputo
Mbabane
SWAZILAND
Maseru
Durban
Bloemfontein
LESOTHO
SOUTH
AFRICA
Cape Town
Cape of Good Hope
Cape Agulhas
Tropic of Capricorn

N
W   E
S

KEY

— National border
⊛ National capital
• Other city

0 miles   1,000
0 kilometers   1,000

▲ A political map of Africa

Workbook

For more practice, go to Workbook pages 7–12.

The World: Political

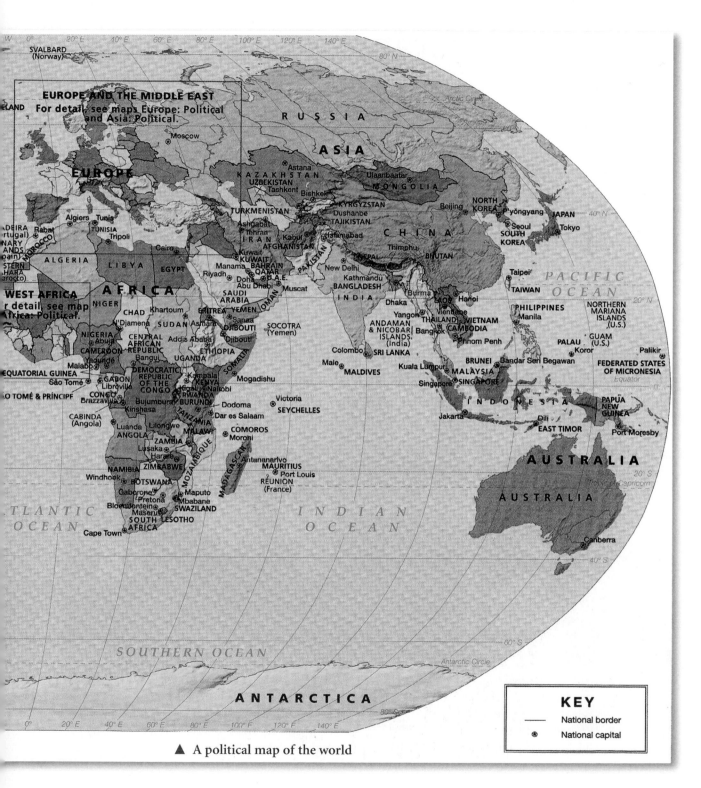

▲ A political map of the world

Using Timelines, Charts, and Graphs

When you study social studies, you see many *timelines*, *charts*, and *graphs*. Timelines, charts, and graphs give you a lot of information in a way that you can easily understand.

- Timelines show what happened over a long period of time.
- Charts use pictures and words to help you compare a lot of things.
- Graphs are pictures that show and compare information.

Timelines, charts, and graphs come in many different forms.

▲ Timelines, charts, and graphs are useful tools to help you learn social studies.

Timelines

A *timeline* shows important events that happened over a period of time. Each important event is listed in the order it happened on the line. A timeline will help you keep track of events that you read about.

Look at the timeline. Read it from left to right. Try to understand how each event relates to other events.

1492 Christopher Columbus's first voyage to the Americas

1528–1536 Cabeza de Vaca explores southeastern North America

| 1490 | 1500 | 1510 | 1520 | 1530 | 1540 | 1550 |

1513–1514 Ponce de León explores Florida

1520 Hernán Cortés conquers the Aztecs

1539–1541 Hernando de Soto explores southeastern North America

Before You Go On

1. Who was the first explorer to come to the Americas? When?

2. Who conquered the Aztecs? When?

3. Did Hernando de Soto explore southeastern North America before or after Cabeza de Vaca?

Charts

A chart uses words to help you understand information. Sometimes charts use pictures, too.

The chart below is divided into columns (the list of words that read from top to bottom) and rows (the list of words that read from left to right). The top row on this chart tells you the title of the chart.

Immigration to the United States by Region, 2004	
Asia	236,039
Mexico	114,984
Europe	102,843
Caribbean	67,660
South America	54,155
Central America	53,435
Africa	45,640
Oceania	5,102
Other	25,965
All countries	**705,823**

The chart below is called a flowchart. This kind of chart shows a process. It can also show a series of events.

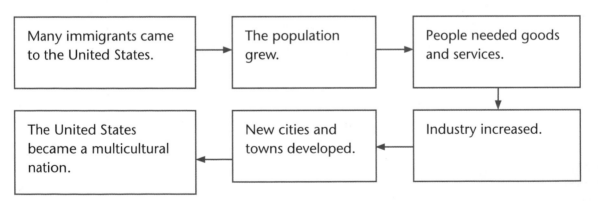

Graphs

Graphs are special kinds of pictures. A graph can show how something changes over time. A graph can also show how one thing compares to other things. Two types of graphs are line graphs and bar graphs.

The line graph below shows the world population between 1800 and 2000. In this graph, the number of people is on the left side (in billions), up and down; the years are across the bottom.

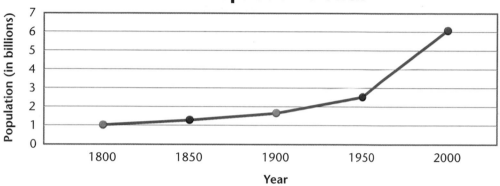

World Population Growth

The bar graph below shows the same information as the line graph, but uses bars instead of a line.

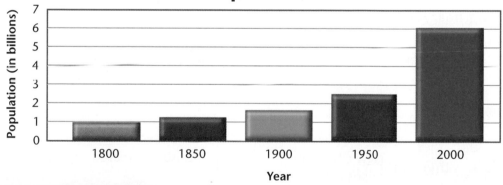

World Population Growth

Before You Go On

1. Look at the chart on page 26. Which region had the most immigrants in 2004?

2. Name two kinds of graphs. How do they show information?

3. What was the world population in 1800? In 1900? In 2000?

For more practice, go to Workbook pages 13–15.

Using Primary Sources

Primary sources are original documents that were written or made at the time events happened. A letter, a sign, a speech, or a newspaper can be a primary source. Even a cartoon can be a primary source. When you read a primary source you can interpret the past. A primary source is a link from the past to the present. History can really come to life.

Primary sources are very interesting. They are the most important tools to use when you try to understand an event. You can also use primary sources to help you answer questions and interpret events that happened long ago.

We must interpret primary sources. To interpret, or to explain or decide on the meaning of an event, ask yourself these questions.

BOYS and GIRLS!
You can Help your Uncle Sam
Win the War

W.S.S.

Save your Quarters
BUY WAR SAVINGS STAMPS

- What is it?
- Who was the author?
- Who is the audience?
- What is the purpose?
- When was it made?

This poster is a primary source. The poster was created in 1917 during World War I. "Uncle Sam" is the nickname of the United States government.

Practice

Look at the poster and answer the questions in your notebook.

1. Who do you think is the author of the poster?
2. What does Uncle Sam want boys and girls to do? Why?
3. What is the purpose of the poster?
4. Who is the audience?

For more practice, go to Workbook page 16.

Reading Social Studies

Reading Strategies

You can have success in social studies if you read, remember, and understand the information. *Reading strategies* can help you. In this book there is a reading strategy before every reading.

- Preview
- Predict
- Visualize
- Ask questions
- Monitor comprehension
- Understand chronological order
- Reread (to monitor comprehension)
- Use selective attention
- Use what you know (background knowledge)
- Look for cause and effect
- Compare and contrast
- Draw conclusions
- Summarize
- Understand fact and opinion

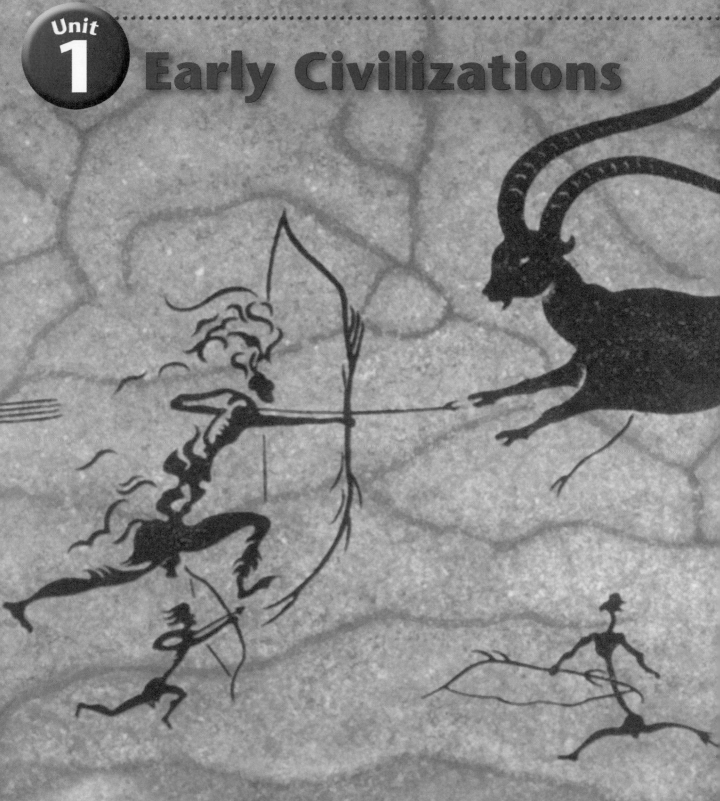

Unit Contents

People

- Hammurabi
- King Khufu
- Hatshepsut
- Shi Huangdi
- Confucius
- Lao Tzu
- Cyrus
- Darius

Places

- Mesopotamia
- Babylonia
- Assyria
- Phoenicia
- Egypt
- The Nile River
- Nubia
- The Great Wall of China
- Persepolis

Key Events

- Discovery of fire
- Development of farming
- Invention of the wheel

Get Ready

What do you already know about early civilizations? Name one civilization and write what you know about it in your notebook.

Vocabulary

Early humans were **hunter-gatherers**. They hunted animals for food and clothing. They gathered plants, seeds, and fruit for food. ▼

▲ This woman is an **archaeologist**. Archaeologists are scientists. They look for places where people lived a long time ago. They look for tools, pottery, and human bones.

A long time ago during the Ice Age, very large areas of ice called **glaciers** covered much of the earth. ▼

▲ Some early humans planted seeds to grow **crops** such as corn. Growing crops and raising animals for people to eat is called **agriculture**. People used the rivers for **irrigation**, or making water flow to dry land. Irrigation from rivers is still used today to water crops.

Key Words

agriculture

archaeologist

crops

glaciers

hunter-gatherers

irrigation

Practice

Choose the word that completes each sentence. Write the sentences in your notebook.

1. A scientist who studies how people lived in the past is an _____.
   a. agriculture   **b.** hunter-gatherer   **c.** archaeologist

2. Early humans who hunted animals and gathered seeds and plants were _____.
   a. archaeologists   **b.** hunter-gatherers   **c.** glaciers

3. _____ are very large areas of ice.
   a. Glaciers   **b.** Crops   **c.** Agriculture

4. _____ are plants, such as corn, that a farmer grows.
   a. Agriculture   **b.** Crops   **c.** Glaciers

5. Making water flow to dry land for crops is called _____.
   a. irrigation   **b.** agriculture   **c.** glaciers

6. _____ is growing crops and raising animals for people to eat.
   a. Hunter-gatherers   **b.** Irrigation   **c.** Agriculture

For more practice, go to Workbook page 17.

Social Studies Skills

Content Reading Strategy: **Preview**

To **preview** means to look at the page before you read to help you understand what it is about. This helps you when you are reading.
To preview:

- look at the page quickly
- look at the **heading**
- look at **vocabulary words** and their meanings
- look at the **picture** and **caption**

Ask yourself these questions:

- What is the text about?
- What do I see in the picture?

Now you already know something about the topic of the page.
You are ready to read.

heading ——
vocabulary ——
caption ——
picture ——

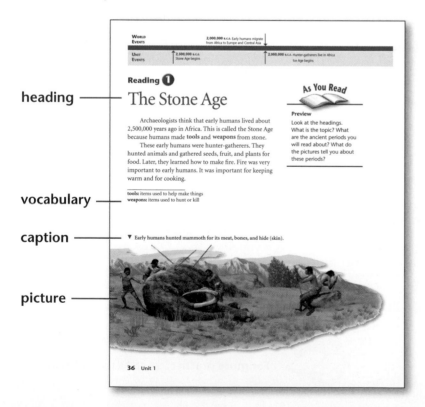

**For more practice,
go to Workbook page 18.**

Using Visuals: **Use a Timeline**

A **timeline** shows years and events in chronological order. Chronological order is the time order in which things happened. The information in the timeline tells us about that period of history.

   Here is a timeline about the history of agriculture.

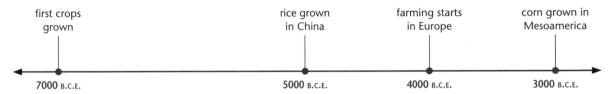

The History of Agriculture

| first crops grown | rice grown in China | farming starts in Europe | corn grown in Mesoamerica |

| 7000 B.C.E. | 5000 B.C.E. | 4000 B.C.E. | 3000 B.C.E. |

1. What event is first on the timeline?

2. What event happened in 4000 B.C.E.?

3. How many years are there between the first and second events?

For more practice, go to Workbook pages 19–20.

Reading ①

The Stone Age

Archaeologists think that early humans lived about 2,500,000 years ago in Africa. This is called the Stone Age because humans made **tools** and **weapons** from stone.

These early humans were hunter-gatherers. They hunted animals and gathered seeds, fruit, and plants for food. Later, they learned how to make fire. Fire was very important to early humans. It was important for keeping warm and for cooking.

___

tools: items used to help make things
weapons: items used to hunt or kill

As You Read

Preview

Look at the headings. What is the topic? What are the ancient periods you will read about? What do the pictures tell you about these periods?

▼ Early humans hunted mammoth for its meat, bones, and hide (skin).

15,000 B.C.E. End of last Ice Age; beginning of Neolithic Period   **14,000** B.C.E. Creation of cave paintings in France

500,000 B.C.E. First use of fire   **10,000** B.C.E. Early humans cross into North America from Asia

The Ice Age

The Ice Age lasted a very long time—from about 2,000,000 to 15,000 years ago. Glaciers covered much of the earth. It was very cold. Early humans had to **adapt** to the cold. They had to protect themselves from **freezing**.

During the Ice Age, the first humans came to North America from Asia. Perhaps these humans followed the animals they hunted. As the earth warmed, the Ice Age ended.

---

adapt: change because of a new situation
freezing: getting very, very cold

> ## MORE ABOUT IT
>
> ### Ice Age Homes
> Early humans made homes out of branches, animal skins, and bones.
>
>

◀ Early humans painted hunting scenes in caves.

Before You Go On

1. How did early humans get their food?
2. Why was fire important?
3. Why do you think early humans painted hunting scenes in caves?

Early Farmers

Early humans started farming in about 7000 B.C.E. This controlled their food sources. Instead of moving around to find food, they stayed in one place and stored crops from one season to the next.

Early farmers planted crops such as wheat and corn. Because crops needed water to grow, people **settled** near large rivers. The farmers used water from the rivers to irrigate their crops. They made irrigation **canals**. The first cities were near these rivers.

---

settled: lived in a new place
canals: long, narrow waterways

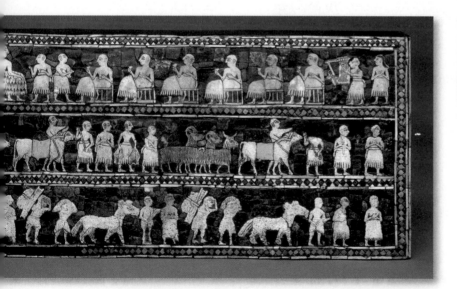

▲ This picture shows farming scenes from daily life.

CONNECT TO
TODAY

Irrigation

Irrigation is very important today. About 39% of all fresh water in the United States goes to irrigating crops. The southwestern part of the United States is a desert and gets very little rain. Farmers must bring the water to their crops. In California, for example, farmers bring more than 30 million gallons of water to 10 million acres of land each day.

6000 B.C.E. Wheat farming spreads in Nile Valley and Africa

Dogs and fowl raised in Mexico and Central America

5000 B.C.E. Rice grown in southeast Asia and China

4000 B.C.E. Farming begins in central Europe and Mediterranean coast

6600 B.C.E. People learn to make bronze

6000 B.C.E. People begin to trade

The Bronze Age

By 6600 B.C.E. people had learned to make bronze. They made bronze by combining two metals: copper and tin. Bronze is much harder than stone. Bronze weapons and tools were better and lasted longer than stone tools. Copper and tin were hard to find in Europe. People had to travel to find them. They met other people in faraway places. They began to trade with these people. They **traded** pottery, tools, weapons, baskets, cloth, and spices. They traded these **goods** for copper and tin. They also traded for food and cloth.

---

traded: bought and sold goods
goods: items bought or sold

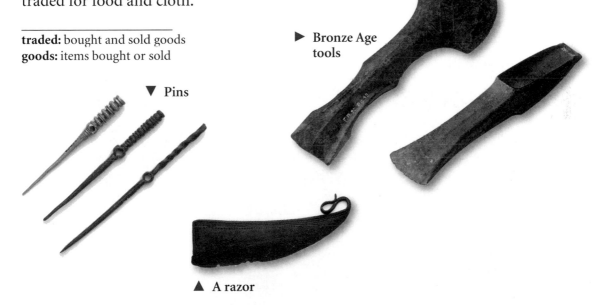

▶ Bronze Age tools

▼ Pins

▲ A razor

Before You Go On

1. Where were the first cities?
2. Why was bronze better than stone for making tools?
3. How did trade change the way ancient people lived?

| WORLD EVENTS | | | | 2600 B.C.E. City of Caral built in Peru | 2500 B.C.E. First libraries built in Egypt |

| UNIT EVENTS | 4000 B.C.E. Babylonian and Assyrian civilizations begin | 3500 B.C.E. Wheel invented | 3000 B.C.E. Sumerians build city-states in southern Mesopotamia | 2500 B.C.E. Assyrians develop battering rams |

Mesopotamia

Mesopotamia was one of the first civilizations. It was where parts of Syria and Iraq are today. The word *mesopotamia* means "between two rivers." The land between the Tigris and the Euphrates rivers was very **fertile**, which allowed people to grow crops. The rivers also supplied fish, reeds to make boats, and clay for building.

In southern Mesopotamia was a region called Sumer. Many Sumerians were farmers. They needed a way to **record** information about their **products**, so they developed a system of writing. The writing was called cuneiform. The Sumerians used cuneiform to write about how they lived. They were the first people to do this.

---

fertile: able to grow things very well
record: write down
products: things people make or grow

MORE ABOUT IT

Invention of the Wheel

Many historians (people who study history) believe the wheel was invented by the ancient Sumerians around 3500 B.C.E. Wheels first appear in ancient Sumerian art. These wheels were made of wood. They were attached to carts and pulled by animals such as donkeys. The wheel made it easier to carry goods from place to place. It also made traveling faster.

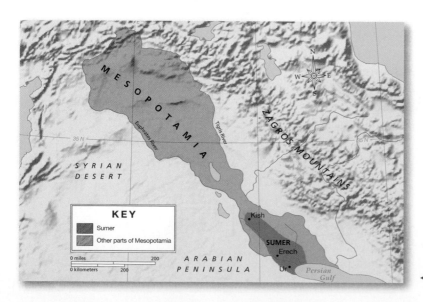

◄ Mesopotamia

2340 B.C.E. Sargon
builds the Akkadian
Empire in Mesopotamia

2300 B.C.E.
Shun dynasty in China

2100 B.C.E.
Akkadian Empire falls

1792 B.C.E. Hammurabi builds
a new empire in Mesopotamia

The biggest and most important civilizations in Mesopotamia were Babylonia and Assyria. The Babylonians were **warriors** and they **conquered** many other lands. Babylonia was also a center for trade. Trading with and conquering other civilizations made the Babylonians rich. One great Babylonian ruler was Hammurabi. He wrote 282 rules for people to follow. He also wrote the punishments for breaking the rules.

Nineveh was the capital of Assyria. It was a city of great learning. It had a huge library.

warriors: people who fight in battles
conquered: took over by force

MORE ABOUT IT

Battering Rams

The Assyrians were great warriors. Many ancient cities had huge walls to protect them from invaders. The Assyrians developed battering rams around 2500 B.C.E. to destroy the city walls of their enemies. They attached large spears to long beams. Then they rammed the spears into the wall, loosening the stones.

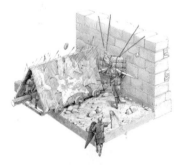

◀ An Assyrian palace

Before You Go On

1. Why was the invention of the wheel so important?
2. What is a battering ram?
3. Explain how people today know about the Assyrian people.

Early Civilizations **41**

WORLD
EVENTS

1500 B.C.E. Ethiopia becomes an independent power

The earliest known settlement established in Mexico

UNIT
EVENTS

3000 B.C.E. Sumerians
create cuneiform writing

Primary Source

Cuneiform

The Sumerians created a system of writing about 5,000 years ago. They wrote on flat pieces of clay. This writing is called cuneiform. The Sumerians used cuneiform to write numbers. Farmers used cuneiform to record facts, such as how many sheep they had. The wedges stood for different numbers.

wedges

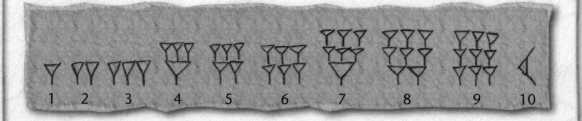

1. What was cuneiform used for?
2. Write the number 12 in cuneiform.

1193 B.C.E. Destruction
of Troy in Trojan War

1100 B.C.E. First
dictionary in China

970 B.C.E. King David reunites
the Israelites and controls Palestine

1200 B.C.E. Phoenician
civilization develops

The Phoenicians

The Phoenicians lived where the country of Lebanon is today. From 1200 to 600 B.C.E., the Phoenicians were great sea traders and explorers. They told stories about sea **monsters** so that other people would be afraid and would not want to **compete** with them for trade.

Writing was important to the Phoenicians. The Phoenician alphabet is the basis of many languages, including English.

---

monsters: scary creatures that are usually huge
compete: try to be better than someone else

◄ A busy Phoenician port

MORE ABOUT IT

Purple Dye

The word *Phoenician* comes from the ancient Greek word *phoinikies,* meaning "purple dye." The Phoenicians were famous for this dye. They made the dye from tiny sea snails. The dye was very expensive to make. Purple became the favorite color of royalty because only kings and queens could afford the dye. No one else wore purple.

Before You Go On

1. Why did the Phoenicians tell stories about sea monsters?
2. How did the Phoenicians make their purple dye?
3. For what other reasons might the Sumerians have used writing?

Early Civilizations **43**

····Lesson ❶····Review and Practice·······

Vocabulary

Choose a word from the box to complete each sentence.
Write the sentences in your notebook.

agriculture	irrigation	crops
hunter-gatherers	glaciers	archaeologist

1. During the Ice Age _____ covered much of the earth.

2. Taking water from the rivers to help grow crops is called _____.

3. Early humans were _____; they hunted animals and gathered seeds, fruit, and plants.

4. The system of growing crops and raising animals to eat is called _____.

5. Early farmers planted _____ such as corn and wheat.

6. An _____ is a scientist who digs up tools, pottery, and human bones to study how early humans lived.

Check Your Understanding

Write the answer to each question in your notebook.

1. Why did early humans settle near rivers?

2. Why was the discovery of bronze important?

3. Why did trade between different areas develop?

4. Why did the Sumerians develop writing?

Apply Social Studies Skills

Content Reading Strategy: **Preview**

What did you learn when you previewed the reading? What did you look at to preview it?

Using Visuals: **Use a Timeline**

Create a timeline in your notebook using the information in the table. Then answer the questions in your notebook.

Ancient Cities		
City	**Present-Day Location**	**Date Founded**
Ur	Iraq	3500 B.C.E.
Memphis	Egypt	2920 B.C.E.
Mohenjo-Daro	Pakistan	2700 B.C.E.
Knossos	Greece	2000 B.C.E.
Anyang	China	1700 B.C.E.

1. What is the title of the timeline?

2. How many years are there between the founding of the cities of Ur and Memphis?

3. What date was Mohenjo-Daro founded?

4. How many years does this timeline cover?

5. What is the present-day location of the city of Ur?

▲ The ruins of Mohenjo-Daro in Pakistan

Discuss

The Sumerians created a system of writing because farmers needed to record facts. Can you think of some inventions today that were created because people needed or wanted to do something?

Workbook

For more practice, go to Workbook pages 21–22.

Vocabulary

A pyramid was a tomb for an Egyptian pharaoh, or **ruler**. ▼

▲ The Egyptians built large **pyramids**. They took twenty years to build and still stand today. They are **ancient**, or very old.

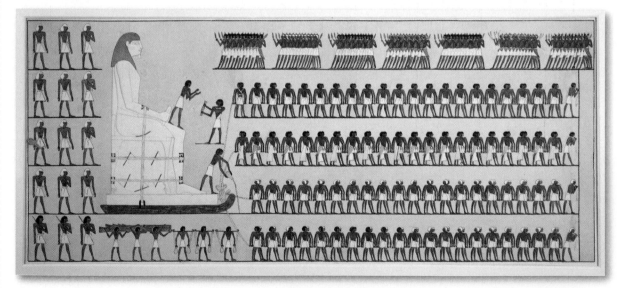

▲ A **society** is a group of people living together. In some societies people lived in separate levels, from richest to poorest. These levels are called **classes**. The lowest class was the slaves. They worked very hard for no money.

Key Words

ancient

classes

invaders

pyramids

ruler

society

◀ **Invaders** are people who go into someone else's country and try to take over by force. Many civilizations built walls around their cities to stop invaders.

Practice

Choose the word that completes each sentence. Write the sentences in your notebook.

1. The separate levels of people in a society are called _____.
   a. pyramids   **b.** classes   **c.** invaders

2. People who come to a country from another place to take over by force are _____.
   a. invaders   **b.** ancient   **c.** classes

3. A _____ is a group of people living together.
   a. classes   **b.** invader   **c.** society

4. _____ are ancient Egyptian tombs.
   a. Society   **b.** Pyramids   **c.** Invaders

5. Something that is very old is _____.
   a. pyramids   **b.** invaders   **c.** ancient

6. A pharaoh was the _____ of Egypt.
   a. ruler   **b.** invader   **c.** society

For more practice, go to Workbook page 23.

Social Studies Skills

Content Reading Strategy: **Predict**

When you **predict**, you try to guess what will happen next.
You use what you already know to help you.

   Look at the picture. Predict what will probably happen next.
Tell a partner three predictions.

Make a chart like this one in your notebook. Fill it in with pictures
or words that describe your predictions.

 For more practice, go to Workbook pages 24–25.

Using Visuals: **Use a Timeline**

Look at the important events in ancient history. Then copy the timeline below into your notebook. Put the events in the correct order on the timeline.

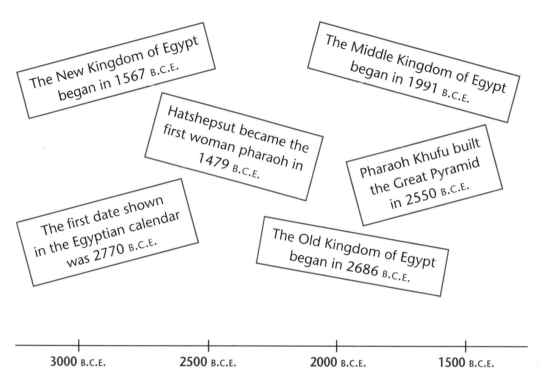

The New Kingdom of Egypt began in 1567 B.C.E.

The Middle Kingdom of Egypt began in 1991 B.C.E.

Hatshepsut became the first woman pharaoh in 1479 B.C.E.

Pharaoh Khufu built the Great Pyramid in 2550 B.C.E.

The first date shown in the Egyptian calendar was 2770 B.C.E.

The Old Kingdom of Egypt began in 2686 B.C.E.

|————————|————————|————————|————————|
3000 B.C.E.   2500 B.C.E.   2000 B.C.E.   1500 B.C.E.

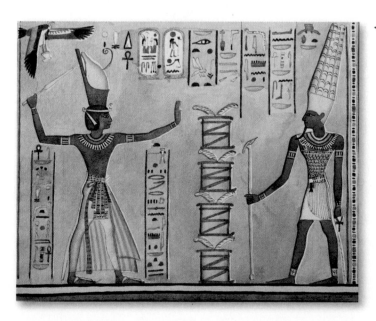

◀ An Egyptian wall painting

For more practice, go to Workbook page 26.

Reading ❷

Ancient Egypt

The ancient Egyptian civilization lasted from 3100 B.C.E. to 332 B.C.E. There were three time periods we call kingdoms: the Old Kingdom, the Middle Kingdom, and the New Kingdom. The Egyptians studied mathematics and science. They learned about medicine and they loved art. Many paintings and carvings were made by Egyptian artists. They still exist today.

MATH CONNECTION

Egyptian Calendar

The ancient Egyptians changed how people counted time. They were the first people to use the 365-day calendar. Their year began on July 19. Every year at this time, the same two things happened. First, the star Sirius appeared in the sky. Soon after, the Nile River flooded. The Egyptians used this calendar to record much of their history.

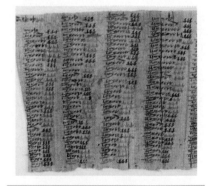

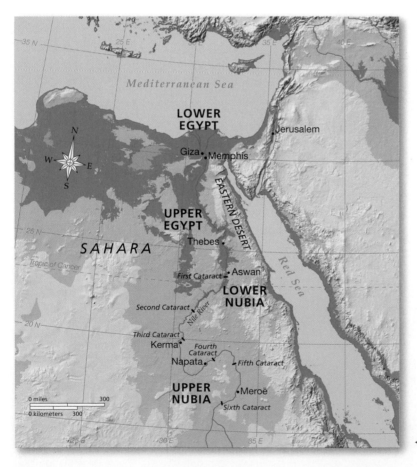

◀ Ancient Egypt and Nubia

The Egyptians wrote with pictures. We call this writing hieroglyphics. Egypt was a class society. Egypt had upper-class, middle-class, and lower-class groups. Most upper-class Egyptians owned slaves. Slaves were the lowest class. The rulers of Egypt were called pharaohs. The people believed the pharaohs had god-like powers. The Egyptians had many gods. They believed that there was life after death.

As You Read

Predict

Look at the map on page 50. Can you predict where the major Egyptian cities will be built?

▲ Hieroglyphics on the wall of a tomb

ELSEWHERE IN THE WORLD

Stonehenge

From 3500 to 1900 B.C.E. people in England built a monument. They placed 80 stone blocks in a circle. Some blocks weighed 26 tons! Today we call this monument Stonehenge. People think it may have been a calendar.

Before You Go On

1. What subjects interested the ancient Egyptians?
2. Why do we know so much about Egyptian life? Give some examples.
3. What objects can you see in the hieroglyphics?

Egyptians **preserved** the bodies of dead people. The dead bodies are called mummies. Workers made a sarcophagus, or **coffin**. Pharaohs had three or four coffins that fit inside one another. Egyptians buried the pharaoh in a **tomb**. Some tombs were inside the pyramids. Egyptians built the largest pyramid in Egypt for a pharaoh named King Khufu. He was about twenty years old when he became pharaoh in 2551 B.C.E.

---

preserved: kept from being damaged
coffin: box in which a body is put before it is buried
tomb: room where a coffin is placed

Profile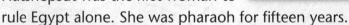

Hatshepsut

Hatshepsut was the wife of a pharaoh, Thutmose II. He died in 1479 B.C.E. Then Hatshepsut's nephew was going to be pharaoh. He was still a boy, so Hatshepsut became pharaoh instead. Hatshepsut was the first woman to rule Egypt alone. She was pharaoh for fifteen years.

While Hatshepsut was pharaoh, Egypt was at peace. Hatshepsut sent ships to other countries to trade. The ships brought back gold, silver, and many other rare things. Hatshepsut was also a great builder. She worked to rebuild many old temples. She also built new temples. One of them still exists today. It is more than 3,000 years old.

MORE ABOUT IT

Mummies

It took about three months to make a mummy. First, Egyptians removed the organs from the body. Then they filled the body with salt and stored it for about forty days to dry out. Next, they cleaned the body and bathed it in spices. Then they wrapped the body in bandages. Finally, they put the body inside the coffin and placed it in the tomb. Sometimes pets such as cats were mummified, too.

970 b.c.e. King Solomon begins his rule in Israel

900 b.c.e. Carthage founded in North Africa

700 b.c.e. Celts move into England

600 b.c.e. Construction begins on Acropolis in Athens

400 b.c.e. Fall of Olmec civilization in Mexico

700 b.c.e. Nubia gains independence from Egypt

Ancient Nubia

Ancient Nubia was the land south of Egypt. Nubia and Egypt traded goods. Sometimes they fought in wars. Nubia's **archers** were very skilled. Egypt ruled Nubia for about 1,000 years.

In the Nubian city of Kerma, people buried their kings in **mounds**. They placed the king's body on top of gold-covered beds **surrounded** by jewelry and other riches.

Around 700 b.c.e. the Nubians got their independence from the Egyptians. But they were invaded by the Assyrians after the Egyptians left. The Nubians moved south to the ancient city of Meroë. They traded goods from Africa for goods from India.

---

archers: people who use bows and arrows
mounds: small hills
surrounded: covered on all sides

LANGUAGE TIP

Possessive Nouns

To show that something belongs to someone, add an apostrophe (') + -s.

Nubia**'s** archers
the king**'s** body

Before You Go On

1. How long did it take to prepare a mummy?
2. Who conquered the Nubians?
3. What do you think happened to the Nubians?

◀ Nubian archers

Early Civilizations 53

WORLD EVENTS

1000 B.C.E. King David
unites Israel and Judah

900 B.C.E. Phoenicians
settle in Cyprus

UNIT EVENTS

1045 B.C.E. Zhou dynasty
begins in China

Ancient China

Ancient China was the largest **empire** in Asia.
When a Chinese ruler died, his son often became the
ruler. When one family rules for many years it is called
a **dynasty**. The Zhou dynasty ruled China from 1045 to
221 B.C.E. It was the longest dynasty in Chinese history.
The Chinese **emperor** was called the "Son of Heaven."
The Qin dynasty ruled China after the Zhou dynasty. The
most famous Qin emperor was Shi Huangdi. He made
many changes in China. He built the Great Wall
of China to keep his kingdom safe from invaders.

---

empire: large area that is ruled by one person
dynasty: powerful family that rules for many generations
emperor: ruler of an empire

▼ The Great Wall of China is more than 4,000 miles long.

> ### LANGUAGE TIP
>
> **Comparatives and Superlatives**
>
> To show that some things are larger or longer than other things, add -*r* or -*st*, or -*er* or -*est*.
>
> | large | long |
> |-------|------|
> | larg**er** | long**er** |
> | larg**est** | long**est** |

The ancient Chinese invented many important things. They had a form of writing that used symbols and pictures. They had irrigation systems that could carry water from rivers to their fields. The ancient Chinese used **coins** for trade.

Many Chinese followed the teachings of Confucius and Lao Tzu. They were famous teachers who believed that all people are important and should be kind to each other. They also taught that people should live in peace with nature. Many people still follow these teachings today.

---

coins: money made of metal

▲ Terra-cotta statues of ancient Chinese soldiers

CONNECT TO TODAY

Acupuncture

Acupuncture is a kind of traditional Chinese medicine. It began thousands of years ago. Acupuncture is used to treat pain and illness. Long thin needles are put in certain points of the sick person's body. The needles stay in for fifteen to thirty minutes.

Today acupuncture is practiced all around the world.

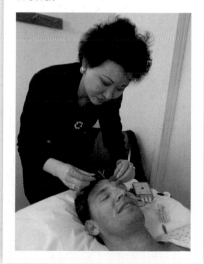

Before You Go On

1. How long did the Zhou dynasty rule ancient China?
2. What did the ancient Chinese use to buy things?
3. What types of ideas did Confucius and Lao Tzu teach? Do you think these are good ideas? Explain why.

Ancient Persia

Persia is the name of an empire that was located where Iran is today. The Persians and the Medes were the two peoples who lived there. The Medes ruled the Persians. The Medes were great warriors. In 551 B.C.E. a Persian chief named Cyrus defeated the Medes and **united** the Persians and Medes into one kingdom. Another Persian king named Darius built a beautiful city called Persepolis. The Persian Empire became very large and ruled over most of the Middle East.

united: made into one group

▲ A Persian palace guard

▼ The Persian Empire

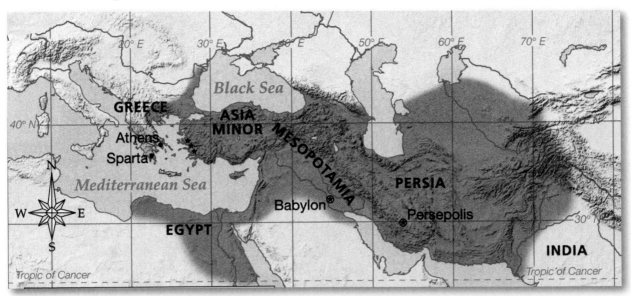

The ancient Persians **worshipped** many gods. The most important god was called Mithras. Mithras was the god of light, truth, and justice. The Persians built great palaces and temples where they worshipped the gods. The Persians **carved** the walls of these buildings with images of famous events from Persian history.

---

worshipped: prayed to
carved: cut into

▲ Persepolis today

MORE ABOUT IT

Persian Cats

Some historians believe that Persian cats were brought from Persia to Europe by Roman and Phoenician travelers in the 1600s. Their long hair protected them in the cold mountainous areas of Persia. The Persians were very fond of cats. They were the pets of kings and believed to have special powers.

Before You Go On

1. Which group of people originally ruled ancient Persia?
2. Who built the ancient city of Persepolis?
3. Why do you think the Persians carved their walls with images of famous events?

Vocabulary

Choose a word from the box to complete each sentence.
Write the sentences in your notebook.

ancient	society	classes
pyramids	invaders	ruler

1. The three levels of people in a _____ were upper, middle, and lower class.

2. An _____ culture is one that existed thousands of years ago.

3. People who take over another country by force are _____.

4. The pharaoh was the _____ of the Egyptian people.

5. Egyptian society had three _____: upper, middle, and lower.

6. The pharaohs' tombs were inside _____.

Check Your Understanding

Write the answer to each question in your notebook.

1. List the classes in ancient Egyptian society.

2. Where did ancient Egyptians bury their kings?

3. What civilization was located where Iran is now?

4. Who built the Great Wall of China?

Apply Social Studies Skills

Content Reading Strategy: **Predict**

Make a prediction about Egyptian farming today based on what you read about ancient Egypt. Choose the best prediction.

- Today in Egypt farmers probably live by the Nile River.

- Today in Egypt there probably are not any farmers.

Using Visuals: **Use a Timeline**

Read the events on the following timeline.

- Which event happened first?
- Which two events have about a thousand years between them?
- What event happened after Queen Hatshepsut died?

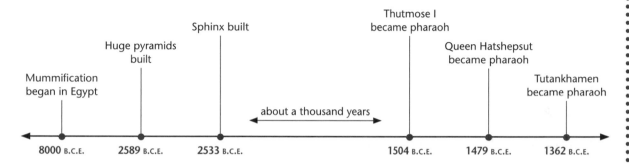

Thutmose I became pharaoh

Sphinx built

Huge pyramids built

Mummification began in Egypt

Queen Hatshepsut became pharaoh

Tutankhamen became pharaoh

about a thousand years

| 8000 B.C.E. | 2589 B.C.E. | 2533 B.C.E. | 1504 B.C.E. | 1479 B.C.E. | 1362 B.C.E. |

▲ Pharaoh Tutankhamen's golden sarcophagus (coffin)

Discuss

Many early civilizations left records of some form of writing. Why do you think languages are so different? In what ways are different languages the same?

For more practice, go to Workbook pages 27–28.

Unit Review

Vocabulary

Choose a word from the box to complete each sentence.
Write the sentences in your notebook.

archaeologist	glaciers	irrigation	classes
agriculture	invaders	hunter-gatherers	crops
ruler	society	pyramids	ancient

1. The _____ Egyptian pyramids are thousands of years old.

2. Ancient farmers planted _____ such as corn and wheat.

3. A scientist who finds out how early people lived is an _____.

4. Large areas of ice called _____ once covered much of the earth.

5. The Egyptians buried their pharaohs inside _____.

6. Early humans who hunted animals and gathered plants for food were _____.

7. Egyptian society's _____ included the lower class, middle class, and upper class.

8. Farmers sometimes use river water as _____ for their crops.

9. Khufu was a great _____ of ancient Egypt.

10. People in Egyptian _____ were divided into different levels called classes.

11. _____ is the system of growing crops and raising animals to eat.

12. _____ sometimes attacked ancient cities.

Timeline Check

Put the events in the correct order. Use the timelines in this unit to help you.
Write the sentences in your notebook.

_____ The Sumerians invented the wheel.

_____ The first farmers settled near large rivers.

_____ The Chinese built the Great Wall of China.

_1_ The earliest humans lived in the Stone Age.

_____ Egyptian kings called pharaohs ruled Egypt.

_____ Hammurabi wrote rules for his people.

Apply Social Studies Skills

Using Visuals: **Use a Timeline**

Make a timeline in your notebook of the important events of your life. Include the year with each event. Put at least ten events on your timeline.

Extension Project

Find out about the ancient city of Knossos in Greece. Explain why you think people like to go there to visit.

◀ Knossos in Greece

Read More About It

Look for these books in the library.

▲ *Early Humans*
by Nick Merriman

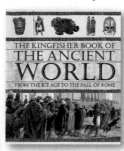

▲ *The Kingfisher Book of the Ancient World*
by Hazel Mary Martell

◀ *Mesopotamia*
by Tami Deedrick

For more practice, go to Workbook pages 29–30.

Writing Skills

Make a Plan

Before writing a paragraph, make a plan. A plan helps you organize your paragraph.

- Think about your topic.

- Make a word web with details about your topic.

For example, this is a word web for a paragraph about the life of Khufu.

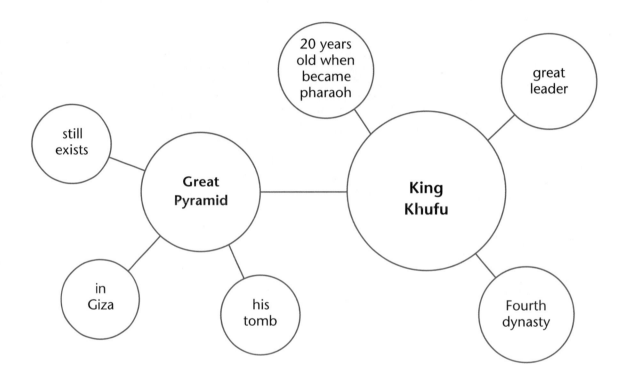

   Here is the paragraph about King Khufu showing the beginning, middle, and end of the paragraph.

King Khufu became pharaoh when he was twenty years old. ⟵ **beginning**
He was a great leader of the Fourth dynasty. Khufu's tomb was
the largest Egyptian pyramid. We call it the Great Pyramid. ⟵ **middle**
People today can still visit the pyramid in Giza. ⟵ **end**

Practice

Look at the word web about Confucius.

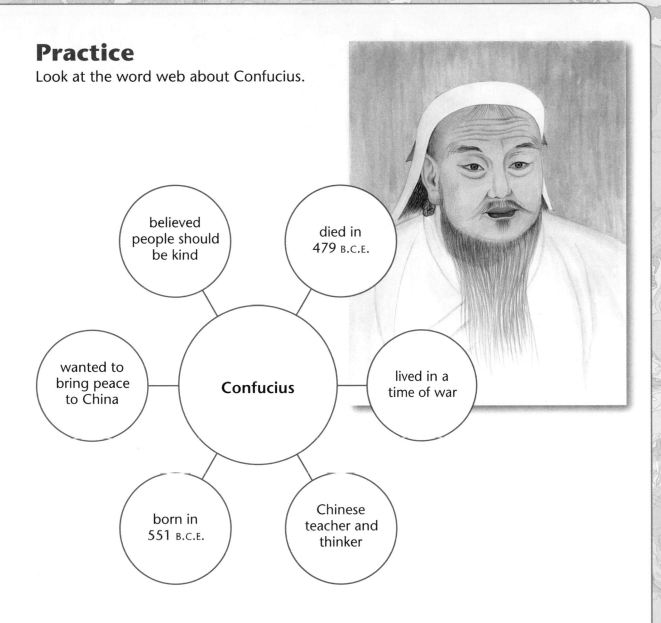

- believed people should be kind
- died in 479 B.C.E.
- wanted to bring peace to China
- **Confucius**
- lived in a time of war
- born in 551 B.C.E.
- Chinese teacher and thinker

Now write a paragraph about Confucius using the word web as a plan. Be sure your paragraph has a beginning, middle, and end.

**For more practice,
go to Workbook pages 31–32.**

The Classical World

Unit Contents

People

- King Tutankhamen
- Cleopatra
- Pericles
- Socrates
- Plato
- Aristotle
- King Philip
- Alexander the Great
- Julius Caesar
- Cato
- Cicero
- Augustus
- Hadrian
- Constantine
- Justinian
- Al-Khawarizmi

Places

- Egypt
- Athens
- Sparta
- Macedonia
- Rome
- Byzantium/Constantinople
- Baghdad

Key Events

- Golden Age of Greece
- Peloponnesian War
- Fall of the Roman Empire

Get Ready

In your notebook, draw a timeline like the one here. Write an event from Unit 1 for each date. Look at page 25 for help.

7000 B.C.E   3500 B.C.E.   2551 B.C.E.   700 B.C.E.

The ancient Greeks made **sculptures**. They used rock called marble to make their sculptures. ▼

▲ The ancient Greeks used clay to make **pottery**. They made jars, jugs, and other everyday items.

Greek artists and builders made **monuments** such as temples to honor their gods. This monument is the Parthenon in Athens. ▼

Key Words

amphitheater

drama

festivals

monuments

pottery

sculptures

▲ The ancient Greeks held **festivals**. A festival is a celebration. A part of many festivals was **drama**, or plays acted out for people to watch. The plays were performed in a large outdoor theater called an **amphitheater**.

Practice

Choose the word that completes each sentence. Write the sentences in your notebook.

1. A _____ is a celebration or feast.
   a. monument   **b.** drama   **c.** festival

2. Figures made of marble or other hard stone are called _____.
   a. sculptures   **b.** pottery   **c.** amphitheaters

3. An _____ is a large outdoor theater.
   a. drama   **b.** festival   **c.** amphitheater

4. A play acted out in a theater is a _____.
   a. pottery   **b.** drama   **c.** festival

5. Everyday items made from clay, such as cups and jars, are called _____.
   a. sculptures   **b.** pottery   **c.** monuments

6. A _____ is a large structure such as a temple.
   a. monument   **b.** amphitheater   **c.** festival

For more practice, go to Workbook page 33.

Social Studies Skills

Content Reading Strategy: **Visualize**

To **visualize** while you are reading means to create a picture in your mind. Visualizing the information on the page helps you:

- understand the words, and
- remember what you read.

For example, in the previous unit you read about some early civilizations. You read about how writing developed. Did you create pictures in your mind?

> Many ancient civilizations developed their own writing. In ancient times people wrote on clay tablets and papyrus (paper made from reeds).
>
> The first libraries began.
>
> We know a lot about ancient civilizations because of their writing.

For more practice, go to Workbook page 34.

Using Visuals: **Use a Map Key**

Maps are drawings of places. They can show a small area or a large area. Maps often use different symbols and colors. The map key tells what each of the different symbols or colors means.

Look at the map of ancient Greece. The map shows cities, mountains, and seas. Look at the map key. The map key explains the symbols on the map. Answer the questions below.

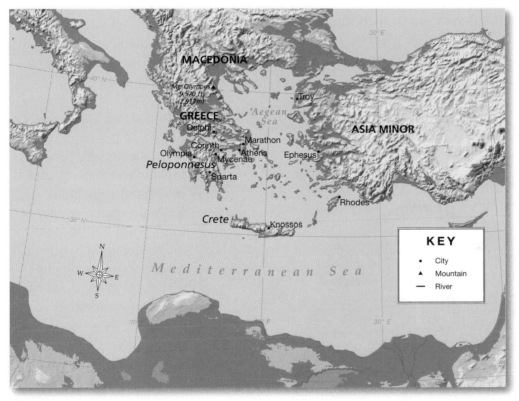

▲ Ancient Greece

1. What is the name of the mountain on the map?

2. What seas are near Greece?

3. Name three cities.

For more practice,
go to Workbook pages 35–36.

Reading ➊

The End of Egypt

The New Kingdom of Egypt began in 1567 B.C.E. Until then Egypt was ruled mostly by invaders. Egyptian princes drove out the invaders and then made themselves pharaohs.

King Tutankhamen was a pharaoh during the New Kingdom. He became the ruler of Egypt in 1336 B.C.E. when he was a young child. He died at the age of eighteen and was buried with many beautiful objects in his tomb.

King Tutankhamen's mask ▼

MORE ABOUT IT

Tutankhamen's Curse

In 1922 a group led by British archaeologists Howard Carter and Lord Carnarvon opened the tomb of King Tutankhamen. They found many treasures, including the pharaoh's beautiful gold mask. Some people believed that a message carved on the tomb wall said, "Death will [come to] whoever disturbs the peace of the pharaoh." Soon after opening the tomb, Lord Carnarvon died. According to one report, six of the twenty-six people at the opening of King Tut's tomb died within ten years. Was there really a curse?

In the year 51 B.C.E., Cleopatra became the queen of Egypt. Cleopatra was Egypt's queen when Roman invaders **conquered** Egypt. Cleopatra poisoned herself with the **venom** of a snake. She died while the Roman soldiers were invading her city. After Egypt was conquered, the Romans became the rulers of the ancient world. Egypt became part of the Roman Empire.

conquered: won control
venom: liquid poison

As You Read

Visualize

Queen Cleopatra chose to die rather than be captured by the Roman army and see her country conquered. Can you visualize these events?

▲ a snake

Queen Cleopatra of Egypt ▼

Before You Go On

1. How did Cleopatra die?
2. Who conquered Egypt?
3. How do you think we learn about other cultures?

The Classical World 71

Early Greek Cities

Early Greek cities were like small countries. Each city had its own **government** and made its own laws. Greek cities were called city-states. Athens was the most important city-state in Greece.

From 500 to 338 B.C.E. life was very good in Greece. Historians call this period the Golden Age. The Greeks created the idea of **democracy**. Pericles was an important leader and warrior in Athens during the Golden Age. He **strengthened** democracy. He made it possible for poor people to be in the government of Athens. He said there should be equal justice for all people.

---

government: the people who control what happens in a country
democracy: a political system where people have the right to vote and choose their leaders
strengthened: made stronger

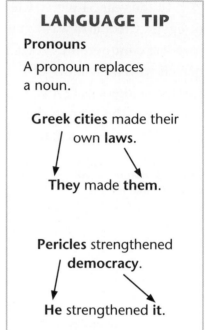

LANGUAGE TIP

Pronouns

A pronoun replaces a noun.

Greek cities made their own **laws**.

They made **them**.

Pericles strengthened **democracy**.

He strengthened **it**.

▼ A Greek home

ladder

roof made of clay tiles

windows with no glass

dining room

hearth for cooking

altar for sacrifices to the gods

walls made of mud bricks

wooden door

Greek Life

Festivals were important to the Greeks. The Greeks held many festivals throughout the year. The Olympic Games began as a festival during ancient Greek times. Greek men liked to discuss politics. They held discussions in the *agora*, or marketplace. Women and slaves were not allowed to vote. Slaves did much of the work in Athens. Some slaves worked on farms without pay for their owners. Some **built** large buildings for the city. Some worked in their owners' homes.

---

built: made

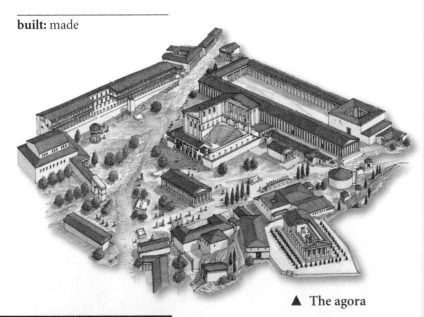

▲ The agora

CONNECT TO TODAY

The Olympic Games

The first Olympic Games took place more than 2,700 years ago in Greece. The earliest date recorded is 776 B.C.E. In the first Games, there were fewer events than today. Only free Greek-speaking men could participate. Women were not allowed to be part of the Games.

The modern Olympic Games began in 1896. The Olympic Games are held every four years in different countries. In 2004 the Games returned to Greece.

AΘHNA 2004

Before You Go On

1. What type of government did Athens have?
2. Who was Pericles and what did he do?
3. How were the lives of men, women, and slaves different?

The ancient Greeks studied science and **philosophy**. The word *philosophy* comes from the ancient Greek word *philosophia*, meaning "love of wisdom." Two important philosophers in Athens were Socrates and Plato. They asked and discussed questions about many things such as justice and courage. Socrates was **put to death** because his questions upset some important people in Athens.

The ancient Greeks were the first people to write plays for the theater. They built large amphitheaters where many people could see the plays.

The arts were very important to the Greeks. Artists made pottery, jewelry, and sculptures.

philosophy: beliefs and values
put to death: killed

▲ An amphitheater

DRAMA CONNECTION

Greek Drama

Ancient Greece was the birthplace of drama, or plays. The word *drama* comes from an ancient Greek word that means "to act." A play is a story that is acted out by people on a stage. Some plays are funny. They are called comedies. Other plays are sad. They are called tragedies.

All the actors in Greek drama were men. They all played more than one character. The actors used masks to show whether the character was happy or sad.

440 B.C.E. Celtic culture spreads from northern Europe to Italy and Asia Minor

430 B.C.E. Hippocrates founds science of medicine

400 B.C.E. Adena people build huge Serpent Mound in North America

432 B.C.E. Parthenon completed in Athens

404 B.C.E. Sparta wins Peloponnesian War against Athens

399 B.C.E. Socrates put to death in Athens

Sparta

The Greek city-state of Sparta did not have a democratic government. Spartan boys began to **train** to be soldiers when they were only seven years old. Spartan girls also had to train to be strong and healthy. All Spartan men had to serve in the army. They had to learn the arts of war. The city-states of Sparta and Athens fought each other for twenty-seven years in the Peloponnesian War. In 404 B.C.E. Sparta finally won the war against Athens.

train: prepare by exercising

▲ Spartan soldiers

ELSEWHERE IN THE WORLD

The Celts

The Celts were a group of people in northern Europe. No one knows much about their culture or religion. We do know that in early Celtic culture, women had important positions. Also, they were very skilled in metalwork. They made beautiful swords, shields, and jewelry. The Celts fought the Romans and Greeks around 440 B.C.E.

Before You Go On

1. Who were Socrates and Plato?
2. How old were Spartan boys when they trained to be soldiers?
3. Would you like to have been a child in Sparta? Why or why not?

WORLD
EVENTS

399 B.C.E. China has political
chaos after the Chin dynasty

360 B.C.E. Crossbow
changes warfare in China

UNIT
EVENTS

359 B.C.E. King Philip takes
control of Macedonia

Macedonia

Macedonia was a state in northern Greece. In 359 B.C.E. King Philip of Macedonia wanted to conquer the city-states of Greece. He built a strong army and succeeded in conquering all of Greece. Macedonia became the most powerful state in Greece. King Philip had a son called Alexander. He trained Alexander to be a soldier. After King Philip was **assassinated** in 336 B.C.E., Alexander became king at the age of twenty.

---

assassinated: killed for political reasons

Profile

Alexander the Great

As a boy, Alexander was very well educated. His teacher was the famous Greek philosopher Aristotle. Alexander also learned to be a good soldier.

After Alexander became king he was not content with ruling only Greece. He wanted to conquer many nations. During a period of ten years, he led his army through Persia, Egypt, Afghanistan, and India. His soldiers admired him because he always fought at the front of the battle. He wanted to spread Greek culture but he also respected the cultures of his enemies. He treated them with respect. He encouraged his soldiers to settle and marry local women. Alexander established many new cities. He became ruler of most of the ancient world.

Alexander died young. In Babylon he got a fever (perhaps from poison) and died at age thirty-two. His empire **declined** after his death. The empire divided into three kingdoms. Three of Alexander's **commanders** ruled these kingdoms. One commander ruled both Greece and Macedonia. One commander ruled Egypt, and the other ruled Persia. The **descendants** of these commanders fought over these lands for the next 300 years.

---

declined: weakened
commanders: people who give orders
descendants: children, grandchildren, great-grandchildren

▼ Alexander during a battle

Before You Go On

1. Who was King Philip and what did he do?
2. Look at the timeline. Where was Chavin culture located?
3. Why was Philip's son called Alexander "the Great"?

Vocabulary

Choose a word from the box to complete each sentence. Write the sentences in your notebook.

amphitheater	drama	festivals
monuments	pottery	sculptures

1. Pyramids and temples are examples of ancient _____ .

2. The Greeks loved _____ such as drama and games.

3. A large outdoor theater is called an _____ .

4. The Greeks made _____ such as cups, bowls, and jugs.

5. The Greeks performed _____ in large amphitheaters.

6. Greek artists made _____ from marble.

Check Your Understanding

Write the answer to each question in your notebook.

1. What kind of government did Athens have?

2. What kinds of art were important to the ancient Greeks?

3. What was life like for Spartan boys and girls?

4. How did Alexander the Great spread Greek civilization?

Apply Social Studies Skills

Content Reading Strategy: **Visualize**

Read this paragraph about Alexander the Great's soldiers. Visualize a picture in your mind as you are reading. Then in your notebook, write three things you remember about the paragraph without looking at it. Remember what you visualized.

> The Macedonian army of Alexander the Great was stronger than any other army. The soldiers used spears and bows and arrows. They also used catapults, which could throw heavy stones or fireballs at the enemy. They had horsemen with weapons. The Macedonians also had a very strong navy with many ships.

Using Visuals: **Use a Map Key**

Look at the map of Alexander's empire. Use the map key to answer the questions in your notebook.

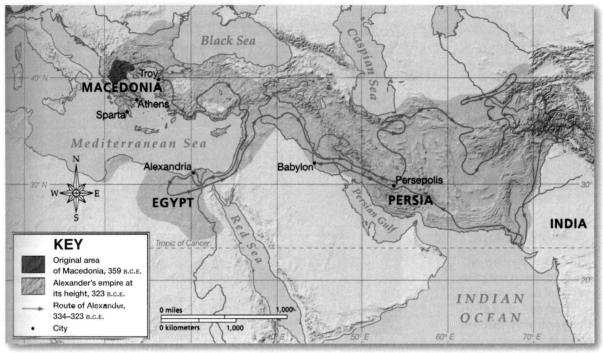

▲ The empire of Alexander the Great

1. What information does the map key give us?
2. Where did Alexander's journey begin?
3. Where did Alexander's journey end?
4. What year was Alexander's empire at its height (most powerful)?

Discuss

The ancient Greeks wrote and performed plays in amphitheaters. Have you ever been to a play? What was it about? Was it a comedy (funny) or a tragedy (sad)?

For more practice, go to Workbook pages 37–38.

The Romans built the **Colosseum**. It held 45,000 people. People watched fights between gladiators and wild animals. ▶

◀ A **senate** is a group of people that makes laws and advises other parts of the **government**.

▼ The Romans built **aqueducts**. Aqueducts are **structures** that bring water into a city.

Key Words

aqueducts

Colosseum

government

prison

senate

structures

▲ A **prison** is a place where people who commit crimes are held for punishment. In ancient Rome people who broke the law were sent to prison.

Practice

Choose the word that completes each sentence. Write the sentences in your notebook.

1. A _____ is a group of people who rules a country.

    a. prison   **b.** government   **c.** structure

2. Buildings and bridges are examples of _____.

    a. senates   **b.** structures   **c.** governments

3. The Romans built the _____ for gladiator fights and other entertainment.

    a. Colosseum   **b.** senate   **c.** aqueduct

4. A place to hold people who break the law is a _____.

    a. aqueduct   **b.** government   **c.** prison

5. The _____ was a group of men who made the laws.

    a. structure   **b.** prison   **c.** senate

6. An _____ is a structure that carries water to a city.

    a. aqueduct   **b.** Colosseum   **c.** government

For more practice, go to Workbook page 39.

Social Studies Skills

Content Reading Strategy: **Ask Questions**

Successful readers **ask questions** before, during, and after reading. Asking yourself questions will help you to understand what you are reading.

Before you read a page, look at the pictures and ask yourself:

- Do I already know something about this?
- How can the pictures help me understand the words?

While you are reading, ask yourself:

- What do I think about this?
- What are the most important ideas I can learn from this page?

After you finish a page, ask yourself:

- Are there any words that I don't understand?
- What do I remember about what I read?

   If you don't understand something, reread the page. Then ask your teacher for help or discuss it with a classmate.

For more practice, go to Workbook page 40.

Using Visuals: **Use a Compass Rose**

A **compass rose** is used to show directions on a map. It is marked north, south, east, and west.

Look at the map of the Roman Empire. The city of Rome was the center of the empire. Use the compass rose to answer the questions in your notebook.

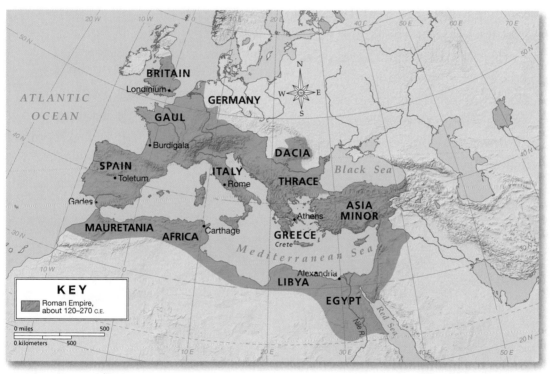

▲ The Roman Empire

1. Which countries are north of Rome?

2. Which countries are south of Rome?

3. Which countries are east of Rome?

4. Which countries are west of Rome?

For more practice,
go to Workbook pages 41–42.

WORLD EVENTS	**814** B.C.E. Phoenicians found Carthage in North Africa	**700** B.C.E. Guayabo Blanco culture flourishes in Cuba	**680** B.C.E. Copper used in East Africa

UNIT EVENTS	**800** B.C.E. First people arrive in area of Rome

Reading ②

The Beginning of Rome

As You Read

Ask Questions

Ask yourself: What do I think about this? What are the important ideas here?

The first people in the area of Rome probably settled there because of the river and the **fertile** land. We do not know much about them except that they arrived around 800 B.C.E. By 264 B.C.E. the Romans formed a kind of government called a republic. In a republic, people choose their leaders by voting.

Roman society included some rich people and many poor people, including slaves. The rich had beautiful villas, or large homes. The poor survived on **handouts** from the government.

1 Atrium
2 Study
3 Bedroom
4 Dining room
5 Kitchen
6 Open courtyard

---

fertile: good for growing things
handouts: money or food
   that is given to someone

A Roman house ▶

480 B.C.E. Persians defeat
Greeks at Thermopylae

300 B.C.E. Euclid
develops geometry

264 B.C.E. Port of Adulis in Ethiopia
becomes center of world trade

264 B.C.E. Romans
form republic

48 B.C.E. Julius Caesar takes
control of Roman Empire

44 B.C.E.
Julius Caesar
assassinated

Rome conquered many nations, and the Roman Empire grew. However, there were many fights within the Roman government.

A strong leader called Julius Caesar took control of the Roman Empire. In 48 B.C.E. he made himself a **dictator**. Many senators did not like this idea, and in 44 B.C.E. a group of senators assassinated Caesar. After the assassination, Rome had a **civil war**. When the fighting ended, Julius Caesar's **heir**, Octavian, became the first emperor of Rome. For the next 500 years, emperors ruled the Roman republic.

---

dictator: one person who rules over a nation
civil war: a fight between two groups from the same country
heir: someone who receives a dead person's money, property, or title

▼ Julius Caesar

CONNECT TO
TODAY

The Senate

The senate was an important part of the Roman government. The members of the senate, called senators, gave advice to the leaders. Many of the early senators, such as Cato and Cicero, were great speakers.

Today, many countries in the world, including the United States, have a senate as part of their government.

Before You Go On

1. Why did people probably settle in the area of Rome?

2. Why did the senators assassinate Caesar?

3. Do you know about any other civil wars? Where and when?

Life after Caesar

Octavian, now called Augustus, died in 14 C.E. Many emperors followed. Hadrian was one of the best emperors. He became emperor in 117 C.E. He tried to build a good government. He made laws to **protect** women, children, and slaves. Many important structures were built while he was emperor. One of the most famous structures is Hadrian's Villa at Tivoli, near Rome.

---

protect: take care of

▼ Hadrian's Villa

CONNECT TO TODAY

Aqueducts

In ancient times, people did not have water in their homes. Aqueducts brought fresh water from the mountains to the cities. People used the water for public baths and fountains.

Today, in desert regions such as southern California, modern aqueducts bring water to big cities like Los Angeles.

4 B.C.E. Jesus
of Nazareth is
born in Judea

77 C.E. Britain
conquered by
Romans

79 C.E. Pompeii
destroyed by Mt.
Vesuvius eruption

14 C.E. Roman emperor
Augustus dies

80 C.E. Colosseum built

117 C.E. Hadrian becomes
emperor

Gladiators were fighters in ancient Rome. They fought each other or wild animals such as tigers. Most gladiators were either slaves or criminals from the prisons. If a gladiator was lucky, he survived to win his freedom.

Gladiator fights were a main form of entertainment for the Roman people. Many gladiator fights were held at the Colosseum. People from all over Rome came to watch.

There were some women gladiators, too. But after 200 C.E., women were not allowed to be gladiators.

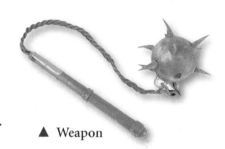

▲ Weapon

▲ Helmet

◄ Roman
gladiators

Before You Go On

1. Why was Hadrian a good emperor?
2. Who were the gladiators?
3. How was Roman entertainment different from entertainment today?

The Classical World 87

| WORLD EVENTS | **105 C.E.** Chinese invent paper | **135 C.E.** Jews exiled from Jerusalem | **220 C.E.** Han dynasty ends in China after 400-year rule |

| UNIT EVENTS | **180 C.E.** Roman Empire declines |

Primary Source

Roman Writing

By the end of the first century B.C.E., the Roman alphabet had twenty-one characters. Later, the Romans added three more. At first, the writing was both from right to left and left to right, changing every line. Then the Romans decided on left to right only.

The writing below is an official government document giving citizenship to certain people. The Romans used writing in business and in government and legal matters. They also wrote letters.

1. Which letters look like letters we use today?

2. How many letters were there in the Roman alphabet?

The Fall of the Roman Empire

Around 180 C.E., the Roman Empire began to **decline** for several reasons. It was too large to defend. The government did not have enough money to pay its soldiers. The emperors were **corrupt** and did not care about the people.

Finally, an emperor named Constantine took control of Rome. Constantine moved the **capital** of the empire to the city of Byzantium, where Istanbul in Turkey is today. He renamed the city Constantinople. After Constantine died, a group of invaders from the north, called Barbarians, conquered Rome.

---

decline: get weaker
corrupt: not honest; cheating
capital: a city that is the center of government

▲ Parts of a sculpture of Constantine

As You Read

Ask Questions

Ask yourself: What do I remember about Greece? How is what I'm reading about Rome different?

Before You Go On

1. Name some reasons why the Roman Empire began to decline.

2. Look at the timeline. Who invented paper? When?

3. The Roman Empire lasted more than 700 years. Why do you think it lasted so long?

The Byzantine Empire

Constantinople was a large center of trade. The emperors who ruled after Constantine remained in Constantinople. Justinian was a Byzantine emperor. He began to rule in 527 c.e. He **established** a fair system of laws called Justinian's Code. From about 900 until about 1050 c.e., the Byzantine Empire was very powerful and its people made many new discoveries. **Scholars** of that time copied important writings from the ancient Greeks. This was the Byzantine Empire's Golden Age.

---

established: started and made happen
scholars: people who study and learn

▼ Hagia Sophia, built as a Byzantine church, is now a mosque.

Chichen Itza

In the late tenth century, a new culture developed in Chichen Itza, Mexico. It was a mixture of Toltec and Mayan people. Chichen Itza was a religious center. The people built hundreds of buildings. One of the most beautiful is the Temple Pyramid called Kukulkán. The Maya-Toltecs left the area in the thirteenth century, but the ruins continue to be important to the Mayan people today.

The Muslim Empire

At the same time as the Byzantine Empire's Golden Age, there was also a Golden Age in the Arabian Peninsula and Persia. Muslim scholars studied mathematics, science, literature, and history. The Muslims conquered many lands, including North Africa, Persia, and present-day Spain. Baghdad was the capital of the Muslim Empire. It was also an important center for trade.

▼ The Byzantine Empire and Islamic world

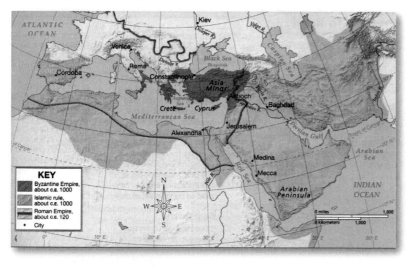

MATH CONNECTION

Al-Khawarizmi

Al-Khawarizmi was a great Muslim mathematician, astronomer, and geographer. He was born in Persia about 780 C.E. He introduced algebra as a way for people to solve problems. He wrote a book called *Al-Jabr wa-al-Muqabilah.* The word *algebra* comes from this famous book. His books were translated into European languages in the twelfth century, introducing this new science to the West.

Before You Go On

1. What was Justinian's Code?

2. Where did the Muslim Empire spread to?

3. Which early civilization would you like to have lived in? Why?

Vocabulary

Choose a word from the box to complete each sentence. Write the sentences in your notebook.

aqueducts	prison	government
Colosseum	senate	structures

1. The _____ advised the leaders and helped to make laws.

2. People who did not obey Roman law went to a _____ .

3. The _____ provided water for the people of Rome.

4. Romans watched the gladiators in the _____ .

5. The Roman form of _____ was a republic.

6. Bridges and buildings are _____ .

Check Your Understanding

Write the answer to each question in your notebook.

1. How were the Romans like the Greeks?

2. Which emperor was assassinated?

3. Why did the Roman Empire decline?

4. What happened during the Golden Age of the Muslim Empire?

Apply Social Studies Skills

Content Reading Strategy: Ask Questions

Reread pages 86–87. In your notebook, write down some questions you asked yourself while you were reading. Write the answers to those questions in your notebook.

Using Visuals: **Use a Compass Rose**

Look at the map of Constantinople during the Byzantine Empire. Use the compass rose to answer the questions in your notebook about directions and location.

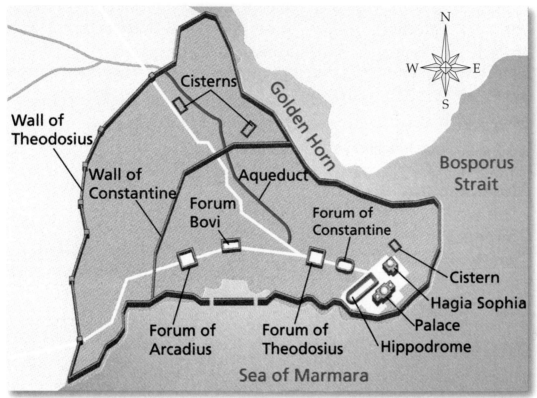

▲ The city of Constantinople

1. What is the name of the sea south of Constantinople?
2. What building is north of the palace?
3. Is the Bosporus Strait west of the city?
4. Are there more forums in the north or south of the city?

Discuss

Gladiator fights were the main forms of entertainment in ancient Rome. What are the main forms of entertainment today? Are there any similarities between what people like to see today and the gladiator fights?

For more practice, go to Workbook pages 43–44.

Unit Review

Vocabulary

Choose a word from the box to complete each sentence.
Write the sentences in your notebook.

prison	government	festivals	drama
monuments	structures	sculptures	amphitheater
Colosseum	senate	aqueducts	pottery

1. The Greeks had _____ to celebrate special events.

2. The Romans built _____ to bring water to their cities.

3. Gladiators sometimes fought animals in the _____.

4. Romans who did not follow the laws were sent to a _____.

5. The Romans built large _____ such as aqueducts.

6. The _____ of Rome was a republic where people voted.

7. People went to the _____ to watch plays.

8. Greek artists made beautiful _____, pottery, and jewelry.

9. The Roman _____ gave advice to the emperors.

10. The Greeks built _____ such as temples to honor their gods.

11. Ancient Greeks and Romans performed _____ in outdoor theaters.

12. The Greeks used clay to make _____.

Timeline Check

Put the events in the correct order. Use the timelines in the unit to help you.
Write the sentences in your notebook.

_____ The first Olympic Games were held in Greece.

_____ Julius Caesar became the dictator of the Roman Empire.

_____ Justinian developed a system of laws in the Byzantine Empire.

_____ The New Kingdom of Egypt began.

_____ Romans formed a republic.

_____ The Greeks created a democracy during their Golden Age.

_____ Constantine took control of Rome.

Apply Social Studies Skills

Using Visuals: **Use a Map Key**

Look at the map of ancient Italy. The map shows where different peoples lived during that time. Answer the questions below in your notebook.

◀ Ancient Italy

1. Where did the Greeks live (north, south, east, or west)?

2. Where did the Etruscans live?

3. Where did the Carthaginians live?

4. In what direction does the Tiber River flow?

Extension Project

Find pictures of artifacts (small objects made and used a long time ago) from Greek and Roman times. Use the Internet or look in reference books. Draw pictures of the items. Write down what they were used for.

Read More About It

Look for these books in the library.

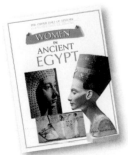

▲ *Women in Ancient Egypt* by Gay Robins

▲ *Ancient Greece* by Anne Pearson

◀ *The Gladiator: A Hero Will Rise* by Dewey Gram (retold by Annette Keen)

Workbook

For more practice, go to Workbook pages 45–46.

Writing Skills

Write a Paragraph

A paragraph is three or more sentences that are written about the same subject (topic).

- Most paragraphs begin with a topic sentence. A topic sentence tells the reader what the paragraph will be about.

- A new paragraph begins with an indentation (a little space before the writing).

- Information needs to be in your own words. Do not copy sentences directly from a book.

   Read the following paragraph about the Roman builders.

   The Romans were very good builders. They built structures that no one had done before. One of the famous buildings was the Colosseum in Rome. They also designed aqueducts. Aqueducts brought water to the city.

   Choose one of these sentences to be a topic sentence for the paragraph above.

- Roman slaves built many structures.

- Examples of Roman architecture exist today.

- The Romans were famous for their excellent architecture.

Practice

Read the following student's paragraph. Change the first sentence so that it is a topic sentence for this paragraph.

> The Muslims became very rich from trading. They conquered many lands. Most of their trading passed through the city of Baghdad. The Muslims had a huge empire.

Now write your own paragraph. Choose one of the people listed on page 65 and write a paragraph about him or her in your notebook. Use your own words. Have a classmate check your paragraph.

For more practice, go to Workbook pages 47–48.

Unit Contents

People

- Justinian
- Muhammad
- Vikings
- Charlemagne
- Samurai
- Genghis Khan
- Marco Polo
- Kublai Khan
- Mayas
- Aztecs
- Cliff dwellers
- Mound builders

Places

- Constantinople
- Mecca
- Medina
- Gaul
- Jerusalem
- Silk Road
- China
- Japan
- Tikal
- Tenochtitlán

Key Events

- Feudalism
- The Crusades
- Bubonic plague
- Invention of gunpowder, the compass, and printing

Get Ready

In your notebook, draw a timeline like the one here. Write an event from Unit 2 for each date.

776 B.C.E	500 B.C.E.	404 B.C.E.	336 B.C.E.	264 B.C.E.

Vocabulary

A **knight** was a soldier. A knight rode on a horse and wore a suit of armor in battle. ▼

▲ **Feudalism** was the type of government that formed during the Middle Ages. It was a class system. The **peasants** served the lords, and the lords served the king. They lived on a **manor**, a large village.

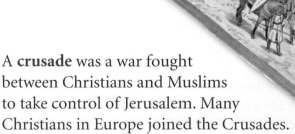

A **crusade** was a war fought between Christians and Muslims to take control of Jerusalem. Many Christians in Europe joined the Crusades. ▶

cathedral

crusade

feudalism

knight

manor

peasants

▲ A **cathedral** is a very large church. During the Middle Ages, cathedrals were built all over Europe for the Roman Catholic Church.

Practice

Choose the word that completes each sentence. Write the sentences in your notebook.

1. A soldier who protected a lord was called a _____.
   a. peasant   **b.** manor   **c.** knight

2. A large village with farms ruled over by a lord was a _____.
   a cathedral   **b.** manor   **c.** feudalism

3. Poor people who worked on a manor as farmers or laborers were _____.
   a. knights   **b.** peasants   **c.** crusades

4. A large church is called a _____.
   a. cathedral   **b.** crusade   **c.** manor

5. A war fought by Christians to control Jerusalem was a _____.
   a. knight   **b.** manor   **c.** crusade

6. A form of government based on a class system was called _____.
   a. crusade   **b.** feudalism   **c.** manor

For more practice, go to Workbook page 49.

Social Studies Skills

Content Reading Strategy: **Monitor Comprehension**

To help you understand a text, a good plan is to **monitor comprehension**. Self-monitoring means checking your understanding as you read.

After you read a paragraph, tell yourself what the paragraph means. If you don't know what it was about, look for clues on the page to help you, such as pictures and definitions. For example, read this paragraph:

> Gothic cathedrals were built during the Middle Ages in Europe. The word *gothic* means a type of architecture. Cathedrals were built in many cities for the Roman Catholic Church. The cathedrals were places for people to pray. Important cities had the biggest and most beautiful cathedrals.

After you read the paragraph and look at the picture, you know the paragraph is about cathedrals built during the Middle Ages. You know why people built cathedrals.

Workbook

For more practice,
go to Workbook pages 50–51.

Using Visuals: **Read a Map**

Maps usually show imaginary lines. These lines are called **latitude** and **longitude**. Latitude lines go horizontally around the earth. Longitude lines go up and down the earth. They meet at the North Pole and the South Pole. The degree symbol (°) is the distance measurement. The equator is 0°, the North Pole is 90°N, and the South Pole is 90°S. Understanding how to use the lines of latitude and longitude can help you locate any place on the earth.

Look at the map, and then answer the questions in your notebook.

◀ Europe in 1400

1. What line of longitude is near the coasts of Portugal and Ireland?

2. What city is located on 0° longitude, 54°N latitude?

3. What line of latitude goes through the middle of Sardinia?

**For more practice,
go to Workbook page 52.**

WORLD EVENTS

543 Nubian Kingdom of Nobatia converts to Christianity

546 Ostrogoths from northern Europe capture Rome

UNIT EVENTS

534 Justinian's Code is finalized

540 Constantinople becomes capital of Byzantine Empire

Reading ①

The Byzantine and Muslim Empires

Around 540 Constantinople became the **capital** of the Byzantine Empire and the largest city in medieval Europe. Justinian, one of the greatest Byzantine emperors, created laws called Justinian's Code. These laws are the basis of the **legal** system of European countries today. The major religion was Christianity. For 200 years after Justinian's death, the Byzantine Empire lost **territory** and power. Ideas and language differences between the Greeks and Romans divided the Church into the Eastern Orthodox Church and the Roman Catholic Church. The Pope was the leader of the Roman Catholic Church.

capital: main city of a country
legal: relating to the law
territory: land

◀ Emperor Justinian (center)

589 Sui dynasty reunites China after 400 years of civil war

600 Hohokam culture emerges in southwest Arizona

604 Prince Umayado creates a new constitution to unite Japan

642 Persian Sassanid Empire falls to Arab invaders

570 Muhammad born in Mecca

622 Muhammad goes to Medina

630 Muhammad returns to Mecca

632 Muhammad dies

In about 570 Muhammad was born in Mecca, a great trading city in Arabia. When he was forty he had a religious experience. He began to **preach** in Mecca, but many people did not listen to his ideas. Some leaders were afraid that he would become too powerful. In 622 Muhammad went north to Medina. The people there listened to him. They believed he was a **prophet**. Muhammad's teachings became the basis of the religion of Islam. His followers are called Muslims.

In 630 Muhammad returned to Mecca. This time, the people supported him. By the time Muhammad died in 632, Islam had spread all across the Arabian Peninsula. Later it spread to North Africa and Spain.

As You Read

Monitor Comprehension
Ask yourself: Do I understand this? Can I tell about it in my own words?

preach: give speeches about religious ideas
prophet: someone who has extraordinary spiritual power

Mecca, a sacred place for Muslims today ▶

Before You Go On

1. What was the major religion of the Byzantine Empire?
2. What was the major religion of the Arabian Peninsula?
3. Do you think the history of religion is important to study?

Primary Source

The Battle of Maldon

During the early Middle Ages, people all over Europe feared the Vikings. In their long ships, they would sail the North Sea. When they landed somewhere, it was to attack.

In 991 an English poet wrote about a Viking attack. A large Viking army had landed in England near the Blackwater River. But the English were ready for the attack. Below is a passage from the story, called *The Battle of Maldon*. It tells what happened when the Vikings first saw the English waiting for them. Stories like *The Battle of Maldon* were told over and over again. They gave people courage in frightening times. As you read, look for words you know. They will help you understand the passage.

Then the Vikings . . . stood on the river bank, [and] cried out loudly [their] message to the earl where he stood on the shore: "Bold seamen have sent me to [you], have commanded me to say to [you] that [you] must quickly send treasure in order to protect [your]self. There is no need for us to destroy one another, if you are rich enough to pay."

. . . The earl, protector of men, [told] a warrior——he was named Wulfstan——to hold the bridge. [They] would not take flight, but defended themselves against the enemy . . .

▲ Vikings

1. What did the Vikings want from the English?
2. What did the English earl decide to do?

839 King Egbert dies after
uniting the Kingdom of England

866 Fujiwara family
takes control of Japan

900 Monte Albán in
Mexico is abandoned

800 Charlemagne
crowned Holy
Roman Emperor

814
Charlemagne dies

Charlemagne

The Middle Ages was the period between ancient times and modern times, from about 500 to about 1500. Western Europe was divided into many small kingdoms. One of these kingdoms was Gaul (modern-day France). Charlemagne was the leader of Gaul. His people were called the Franks. In 768 Charlemagne became King of the Franks.

Charlemagne united Europe for the first time since the Roman Empire. In 800 the Pope made him emperor. Charlemagne ruled as king, then emperor, for nearly fifty years. He improved the life of his people and spread the Christian religion. When he died, his empire declined. Vikings attacked for the next 300 years. Charlemagne's empire was gone and Europe was again divided into many small kingdoms.

▼ Charlemagne

ELSEWHERE IN THE WORLD

Pala Dynasty

The Pala dynasty had power in Bihar and Bengal in India from 765 to 1200. It was called the Pala dynasty because all the rulers' names ended in *Pala,* which means "protector." The Pala dynasty built many Buddhist temples. Many beautiful stone and metal sculptures survive from this period.

Before You Go On

1. What changes did Charlemagne make in Europe?
2. Why did Charlemagne's empire fall apart?
3. Why is this period called the Middle Ages?

The Manor System

After Charlemagne's death, life was more dangerous in Europe because the government was **unstable**. To return order to society, a new system of government called feudalism was developed. In the feudal system, kings and lords owned land and ruled over **vassals**. Kings and lords gave land to their vassals. In return, vassals raised armies and protected the **nobles**. Armies were made up of soldiers called knights.

---

unstable: likely to fall apart

vassals: people who held land for their king or lord in exchange for protection

nobles: people with a royal background, such as lords, barons, and princes

Knights

Knights wore a metal covering called armor to protect them in battle. They followed rules of behavior, called *chivalry*, that were very important. A knight was supposed to be brave in battle, loyal, kind, and humble. Today, "a knight in shining armor" means a rescuer, someone who helps you in a difficult situation.

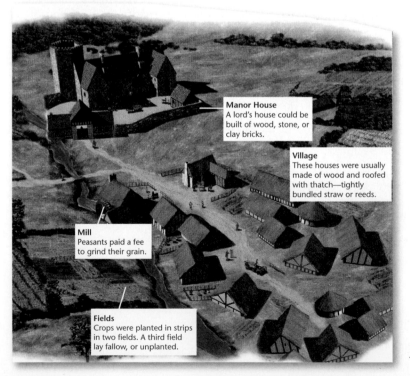

Manor House
A lord's house could be built of wood, stone, or clay bricks.

Village
These houses were usually made of wood and roofed with thatch—tightly bundled straw or reeds.

Mill
Peasants paid a fee to grind their grain.

Fields
Crops were planted in strips in two fields. A third field lay fallow, or unplanted.

◀ A manor

940 Liao dynasty founded in China

962 German King Otto becomes Holy Roman Emperor

979 Tien Le dynasty begins in Vietnam

990 Kingdom of Ghana controls salt and gold trade in western Africa

999 Kingdom of Chichen Itza founded in Mexico

987 Hugh Capet becomes King of France and begins new dynasty

Most people in the Middle Ages were peasants. They were the poorest people in the feudal system. Peasants lived and worked on the manors. Manors were large villages with farms and **pastures**. The lord of the manor was usually a vassal of the king. A vassal depended on his manor to provide **wealth**.

The peasants on the manor were called serfs. Serfs belonged to the vassal. They farmed the fields of the manor. They gave most of the **harvest** to their vassal and kept some for themselves. Some serfs made enough money to buy some land and become free.

---

pastures: large grass fields where animals graze
wealth: a lot of money
harvest: crops such as corn

▼ Peasants working in a field

Before You Go On

1. What was a vassal? What was a peasant (or serf)?
2. Who did a serf belong to?
3. Do you think the feudal system was a fair system?

**WORLD
EVENTS**

1000 Polynesians settle in New Zealand
after 500-year migration

**UNIT
EVENTS**

1071 Turks defeat Byzantine
Emperor Romanus IV

1095 Pope Urban II calls
for crusade against Muslim
Turks to capture Jerusalem

The Crusades

In the 1000s, Muslim Turks took control of the city of Jerusalem in the Middle East. Jerusalem was a **sacred** place for Christian **pilgrims**. The Muslim Turks sometimes attacked the pilgrims on their way to Jerusalem. Then they closed the route to Jerusalem altogether. The Muslim Turks also conquered much of the Byzantine Empire. The emperor in Constantinople asked the Pope in Rome for help. The Pope sent a message to the people of Europe to travel to Jerusalem to fight the Muslim Turks.

Over the next 200 years, the Church sent eight **expeditions** to Jerusalem to try to take back the city. These expeditions are called the Crusades.

---

sacred: holy
pilgrims: people who travel to a holy place
expeditions: long, difficult trips

ART CONNECTION

Stained Glass

The cathedrals and churches built during the Middle Ages had large windows with beautiful pictures. Artists created these pictures using colored, or stained, glass. The windows often showed scenes or stories from the Bible or the lives of saints.

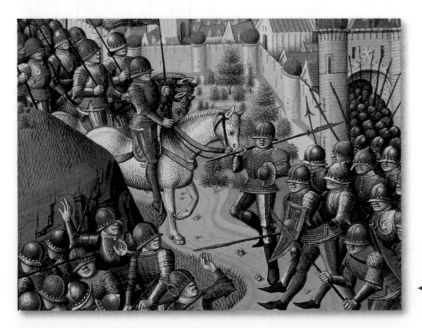

◀ Crusaders marching toward Jerusalem

The Growth of Cities

The Crusades encouraged trade. At first, people traded with each other. Then, as trade grew with other countries, the marketplaces grew bigger. They became towns. Manors could not feed everyone who lived on them, so people moved off the manors and lived in towns along trade **routes**. By about 1300 many towns had grown into cities. The cities grew fast.

Muslim Arabs knew many things about mathematics and medicine. The Crusaders brought this knowledge back to Europe. Technology improved. Europeans learned to make better maps and ships.

---

routes: roads or rivers people use to travel

▲ A medieval town

MORE ABOUT IT

The Black Death

In the 1340s, a terrible disease swept across Europe. The Bubonic plague caused black lumps, or *buboes,* to break out all over the victim's body. Over a period of four years, the plague killed one-third of Europe's population, or about 25 million people. What caused the plague? Cities in the Middle Ages were full of rats. The fleas on the rats spread the disease to humans.

Before You Go On

1. Why did the Crusaders go to Jerusalem?
2. Why did people move to towns?
3. Are there any diseases like the Bubonic plague today?

The Middle Ages **111**

····Lesson ❶····Review and Practice········

Vocabulary

Choose a word from the box to complete each sentence. Write the sentences in your notebook.

knight	peasants	cathedral
manor	feudalism	crusade

1. Vassals protected the lord of the _____.

2. A _____ is a very big church.

3. The _____ were the poorest people in the feudal system.

4. The armor that a _____ wore protected him in battle.

5. Kings, vassals, and knights were in a system called _____.

6. A _____ was a war between Christians and Muslims.

Check Your Understanding

Write the answer to each question in your notebook.

1. Who was Charlemagne?

2. Why did the Crusaders go to Jerusalem?

3. Why did towns grow into cities?

4. How did the Bubonic plague spread?

Apply Social Studies Skills

Content Reading Strategy: Monitor Comprehension

Read the following paragraph about chivalry. Think about what you know about chivalry as you read.

Chivalry was practiced during the Middle Ages. Chivalry was the code that knights lived by. Chivalry meant honor, bravery, and respecting women. Poets and musicians traveled throughout Europe, talking and singing about the bravery of knights in shining armor.

Write what chivalry means in your own words in your notebook. Do you think chivalry exists today?

112 Unit 3

Using Visuals: **Read a Map**

Look at the map. Then answer the questions about longitude and latitude in your notebook.

▼ The routes of the Crusades

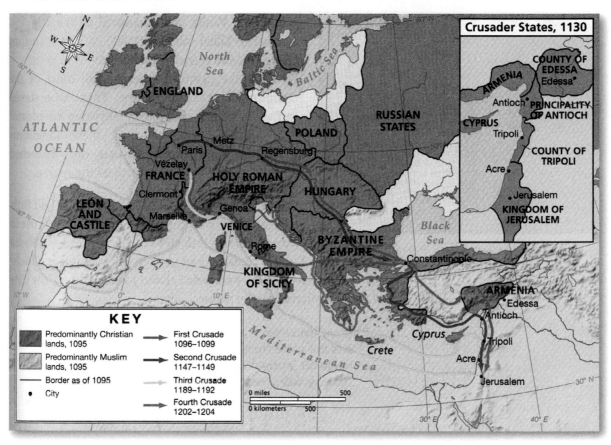

1. Find Jerusalem on the map. Which line of latitude is it near?

2. What city is located at about 28° longitude, 41° latitude?

3. Estimate where Rome is in degrees of longitude and latitude.

Discuss

Do you think the peasants had a hard life? Do you think their lives improved when they moved to the cities? Why or why not?

**For more practice,
go to Workbook pages 53–54.**

Vocabulary

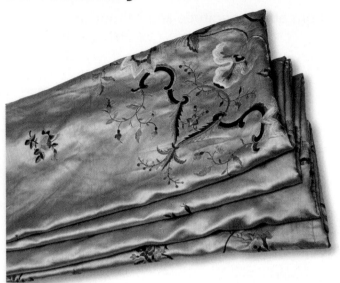

This is a **samurai** warrior from Japan. Samurais were trained to show no fear of death. ▼

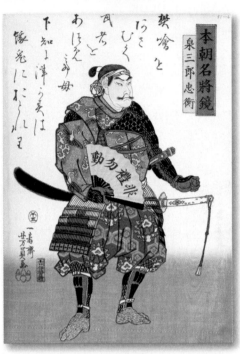

▲ China began to **trade** items such as **silk** with other parts of the world. Trade is when people buy and sell goods. Silk is made from a soft fiber produced by silkworms.

▲ The Chinese built waterways called canals. A **canal** is used for irrigation and for boats and ships to pass through.

▲ During the Middle Ages, dynasties ruled in Japan and China. In a **dynasty**, different emperors come from the same family.

Key Words

canal

cliff dwellers

dynasty

samurai

silk

trade

▲ A group of people in the southwestern United States made their home under cliffs. They were called **cliff dwellers**. The cliff dwellers also built canals.

Practice

Choose the word that completes each sentence. Write the sentences in your notebook.

1. A warrior from Japan who was trained to show no fear of death was a _____.
   a. cliff dweller   **b.** dynasty   **c.** samurai

2. The process of buying and selling goods and products is called _____.
   a. canal   **b.** cliff dweller   **c.** trade

3. Ancient people who made their homes under cliffs were _____.
   a. cliff dwellers   **b.** silk   **c.** dynasty

4. A waterway that is built by humans in order to move ships is called a _____.
   a. dynasty   **b.** canal   **c.** samurai

5. The thin thread or fabric made from the secretions of silkworms is _____.
   a. trade   **b.** silk   **c.** canal

6. A group of rulers who come from the same family is called a _____.
   a. dynasty   **b.** silk   **c.** trade

For more practice, go to Workbook page 55.

Social Studies Skills

Content Reading Strategy: **Understand Chronological Order**

Dates tell when events happened, when people lived and died,
when empires rose and fell. The order or sequence of events is called
chronological order. Timelines show chronological order. In a text, look
for dates and these words: *first, began, later, now, then, before, after,* and
finally.

Read the following paragraph and think about the chronological order
of events.

When people think about exploring or invading faraway places, <u>first</u>
they decide why they are going. <u>Then</u> they decide if is reasonable to go.
For example, Charlemagne wanted to have more land. <u>Before</u> he attacked,
Charlemagne made sure he had enough soldiers, horses, and weapons. <u>Then</u>
in <u>768</u> he invaded a nearby kingdom. <u>Soon</u> he invaded more and more
kingdoms. <u>After</u> Charlemagne conquered most of western Europe, he ruled
the conquered people well. In <u>814</u> Charlemagne died. The <u>last</u> part of his
story is that his sons <u>finally</u> lost most of the kingdom Charlemagne had won
because they did not work together to keep it.

First	Then	Before	Then	Soon	After	Last	Finally
760	770	780	790	800	810	820	830

Workbook

**For more practice,
go to Workbook pages 56–57.**

Using Visuals: **Use a Map Scale**

A **map scale** shows the real distance the map represents. For example, the scale on this map tells you that $1\frac{1}{4}$ inches = 1,000 miles and $\frac{3}{4}$ inch = 1,000 kilometers.

Look at the map scale to answer the questions below. Write the answers in your notebook.

▼ Civilizations of Asia

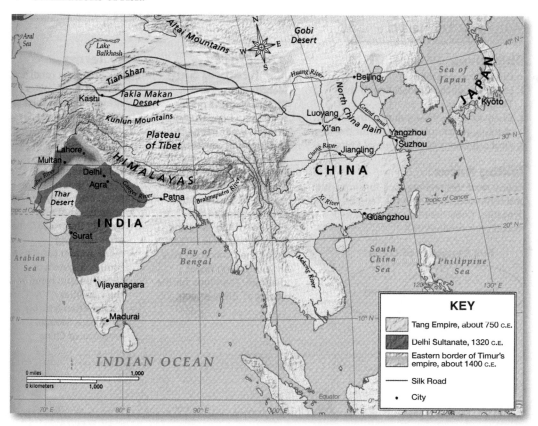

1. Find the trade routes called the Silk Road. Use the map scale to estimate the distance in miles between Kashi and Xi'an.

2. Use the map scale to estimate how big Japan is from north to south.

3. About how many miles is it from Delhi in India to Beijing in China?

For more practice, go to Workbook page 58.

WORLD
EVENTS

614 Persian Empire invades
Damascus and Jerusalem

732 Arabs are defeated
at the Battle of Tours,
present-day France

828 Founding of
St. Mark's Church
in Venice

UNIT
EVENTS

618 Tang
dynasty rules

649 Emperor
Tang Taizong dies

Reading ❷

China in the Middle Ages

The Tang dynasty ruled China from 618 to 907. During that time, China built a 1,000-mile-long canal that connected the Huang and Chiang rivers. The Grand Canal connected southern and northern China. A man named Tang Taizong was a great ruler during the Tang dynasty. He followed the wise and peaceful teachings of Confucius and helped **reform** China's government.

reform: make better

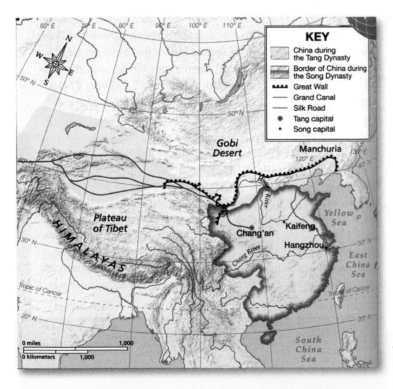

◀ China during the Tang and Song dynasties

CONNECT TO TODAY

The Panama Canal

In 1882 the French began to build a huge canal through the country of Panama. They wanted to connect two oceans—the Atlantic and the Pacific. It was not an easy job. The French had problems with disease, mud slides, and floods. About 20,000 workers died. Finally, the United States finished the project and the canal opened in 1914.

By 960 the Song dynasty ruled China. They changed the government. They **valued** art, books, and beautiful objects. For a long time, only the Chinese knew how to make silk. For hundreds of years Chinese artists made the finest kinds of clay dishes and figures. **Porcelain** and silk were traded. There were many great inventions during both dynasties, such as gunpowder, the compass, and the printing press.

valued: thought was important
porcelain: hard, white material used to make plates, cups, etc.

▼ The world's oldest printed book

SCIENCE CONNECTION

Silkworms

Silk-making in China began more than 3,000 years ago. Women collected cocoons from caterpillars called silkworms. Cocoons are the covering that caterpillars make to protect themselves.

The women carefully separated the silk threads of the cocoons. Then they twisted them together to make yarn. From the yarn the women made fabric on a loom. Silk was very beautiful and expensive. The Chinese kept their method of silk-making a secret for a long time.

Before You Go On

1. What is the purpose of a canal?
2. Name some Chinese inventions.
3. Why do you think silk was so expensive?

WORLD EVENTS

1255 Sundiata Keita, founder of Mali Empire, dies

UNIT EVENTS

1218 Genghis Khan leads Mongol invaders into Turkestan and Afghanistan

1227 Genghis Khan dies

1254 Marco Polo born

1260 Kublai Khan becomes ruler of Mongol Empire

The Mongol Empire

The Mongols were **nomads**. They were also great horsemen and **fierce** warriors. By the 1200s they had a large army. Their leader was Genghis Khan. He created a great empire. The Mongols conquered Russia, eastern Europe, Korea, and northern China. Only the southern Song Empire in China was able to **resist** the Mongols.

LANGUAGE TIP

northern

western ← → eastern

southern

nomads: people who travel from place to place
fierce: angry; ready to attack
resist: hold back

Profile

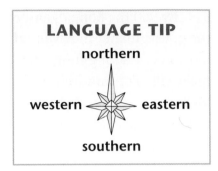

Marco Polo

Marco Polo was born in Venice, Italy, in 1254. His father, Nicolo, and his uncle, Maffeo, were traders. In 1271 Nicolo and Maffeo made a trip east to China. They took 17-year-old Marco Polo with them.

Marco Polo worked for Kublai Khan for many years. He sailed home in 1288. He brought ivory, jade, jewels, porcelain, and silk back to Venice. He told about the Chinese use of coal, money, and compasses. Later, he wrote about his trip in a book called *The Book of Travels*. Marco Polo became famous for his travels through Central Asia and China. His book gave Europeans some of their earliest information about China.

Many people in Europe read Marco Polo's book. Some did not believe his stories of Chinese riches and inventions. In 1324, when Marco Polo was near death, a priest entered his room. The priest asked Marco Polo if he wanted to admit his stories were false. Instead, Marco Polo said, "I do not tell half of what I saw because no one would have believed me."

1325 Tenochtitlán founded
by Aztecs in Mexico

1348 Black Death
kills millions of
people in Europe

1294
Kublai Khan dies

1368 Chinese peasant leads
uprising to overthrow Mongols

Kublai Khan, the grandson of Genghis Khan, became ruler in 1260. He overthrew the Song dynasty. Kublai Khan was now emperor of China. Visitors from many lands came to his court. One of them, Italian trader Marco Polo, wrote about Kublai Khan's beautiful palace. Trade increased between China and Europe. China **prospered**. But after Kublai Khan's death, China declined. In 1368 a Chinese peasant led an uprising that overthrew the Mongols.

---

prospered: became rich and successful

▼ **Marco Polo visits Kublai Khan**

Before You Go On

1. What kind of people were the Mongols?
2. Who became the ruler of the Mongol Empire in 1260?
3. Why do you think Kublai Khan was interested in visitors from other lands?

Japan in the Middle Ages

Japan is a country made up of islands. For a long time, the sea protected Japan from invaders. From 794 to 1185 Japan was ruled by the Heian Empire. The ancient capital was Kyoto. By 1000 feudalism was the way of life in Japan. Peasants worked for nobles. Some nobles hired warriors, called *samurai*, to defend them. Samurai warriors were very skilled fighters. Like knights, they had a strict code of honor. A samurai warrior could not **surrender** to an enemy.

---

surrender: give up

CONNECT TO TODAY

Martial Arts

Kendo is the traditional martial art of fencing, or fighting with swords. The samurai developed kendo in the Middle Ages. Jujitsu is another Japanese martial art based on throws and locks to control an attacker. Both of these martial arts are still popular today.

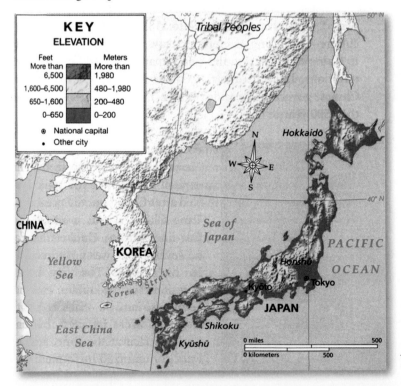

◄ Japan

Samurai warriors were members of **clans**. Each clan was **loyal** to a powerful warlord called a *daimyo*. Samurai warriors promised to die for the daimyo. Small wars broke out between the clans. The most powerful clan was the Minamoto clan. The emperor gave the title *shogun* to the leader of the Minamoto clan. He gave the shogun the power to rule Japan. The shogun protected Japan by keeping foreigners out of the country. Kublai Khan tried and failed to invade Japan. Shogun rule lasted until 1867.

---

clans: groups
loyal: faithful; trustworthy

▼ Samurai warrior

MORE ABOUT IT

The Shogun

Shoguns were military leaders who had unlimited powers. They controlled large armies. Minamoto Yoritomo (1147–1199) was the first shogun to put the whole of Japan under shogun power. Yoritomo had the help of his half-brother and cousins to lead the armies. The shogun system lasted for 700 years.

Before You Go On

1. What two countries are close to Japan?
2. What is a samurai?
3. Compare the code of a samurai to the code of a knight.

WORLD
EVENTS

500 Huns invade
India and Persia

642 Sassanid Empire in Persia
conquered by Muslim Arabs

UNIT
EVENTS

600 Mayan city of Tikal has
nearly 50,000 inhabitants

700 Mound builders
live in eastern North America

Early Civilizations of the Americas

There were many great civilizations in Mesoamerica, the area between modern-day central Mexico and northern Costa Rica. The Mayas lived in Mesoamerica from about 250. They built great cities, such as Tikal in modern-day Guatemala. They developed a calendar and invented a written language. They were very successful farmers. In about 900 the Mayas **abandoned** their cities. No one knows why.

The Aztecs lived from the 1100s in the area where Mexico City is today. Their capital was Tenochtitlán. They built a large empire. By the 1470s, they had conquered the lands around them. They ruled until the Spanish invaded in 1519.

---

abandoned: left

MORE ABOUT IT

Mayan Calendars

The Mayas used three different calendars. One calendar, called the Long Count, is a continuous record of days beginning on August 13, 3114 B.C.E. The sacred calendar used for religious events is called Tzolkin, and the civil calendar is called the Haab. The Haab calendar had 360 days, followed by five extra days. The five extra days were thought to be bad luck days. Other groups such as the Aztecs adopted the Mayan calendar.

◄ The ruins of the Mayan city of Tikal

From about 700 to 1250, a Native American group called the mound builders lived in the eastern half of the United States. They built large and small **mounds** made of piles of earth. Some mounds have nothing in them. Other mounds have human bones, weapons, tools, and art objects.

The Anasazi, or "ancient ones," lived in the southwest United States from about 100 to about 1300. They were cliff dwellers—they built their homes under **cliffs**. They also built canals and grew food and cotton. When **droughts** hit the area, the Anasazi abandoned their dwellings.

As You Read

Understand Chronological Order

Look at the time periods the different civilizations lived in. List them in chronological order.

---

mounds: small hills
cliffs: high, steep rock at the side of a mountain
droughts: long periods of time when no rain falls

◄ Serpent Mound in Ohio

Before You Go On

1. What did the Mayas invent?
2. What types of things do mounds have inside of them?
3. Why do you think the Anasazi built their homes under cliffs?

Vocabulary

Choose a word from the box to complete each sentence. Write the sentences in your notebook.

silk	samurai	cliff dwellers
trade	canal	dynasty

1. The _____ built their homes on the sides of mountains.

2. The Chinese built a _____ that was 1,000 miles long.

3. The _____ warriors had a code of honor similar to knights.

4. Many beautiful garments are made of _____.

5. Marco Polo's stories about China increased _____.

6. A _____ is a group of rulers who come from the same family.

Check Your Understanding

Write the answer to each question in your notebook.

1. What two rivers were connected by the Grand Canal in China?

2. How did Europeans learn about China?

3. Explain what the life of a samurai warrior was like.

4. Where were the early civilizations of the Americas?

Apply Social Studies Skills

Content Reading Strategy: **Understand Chronological Order**

Read the following paragraph about the Heian Empire. Look for dates and words that will help you to put events in chronological order.

> The Heian period of Japan began in 794. Before this time, Japan's culture and traditions were like China's. In the 800s Japan began to develop its own culture and traditions. After 894 Japan and China did not communicate as they did before. This lasted for 500 years.

Now write the above paragraph in your notebook. Then underline the words and dates that help you understand chronological order.

Using Visuals: **Use a Map Scale**

Look at the map below. Use the map scale to answer the questions in your notebook.

▼ Civilizations of the Americas

1. About how many miles is Tenochtitlán from Chaco Canyon?

2. About how far is Cuzco from the most southern part of South America?

3. Which river is longer, the Mississippi or the Amazon?

Discuss

You have read about some early civilizations. Why do you think some civilizations ended?

For more practice, go to Workbook pages 59–60.

Unit Review

Vocabulary

Choose a word from the box to complete each sentence. Write the sentences in your notebook.

silk	samurai	cliff dwellers	knight
manor	feudalism	peasant	cathedral
crusade	trade	canal	dynasty

1. Christians traveled to Jerusalem to fight in a _____.

2. Marco Polo helped increase _____ between Europe and China.

3. A _____ wore armor when he went to war.

4. The Chinese kept their method of _____-making a secret.

5. A _____ worked very hard on the land of a lord.

6. Boats and ships can pass through a _____.

7. The windows of a _____ were made of stained glass.

8. The people who made their homes under cliffs were the _____.

9. The system of government during the Middle Ages was _____.

10. The Tang _____ lasted 300 years in China.

11. Each _____ warrior promised to be loyal to a daimyo.

12. A _____ was a large village where the lord, vassals, and serfs lived.

Timeline Check

540	768	960	1260

Here is a timeline with dates marked on it. Copy the timeline into your notebook and match each event listed below with the correct date.

- Kublai Khan becomes the ruler of the Mongol Empire.

- The Song dynasty takes control of China.

- Charlemagne becomes King of the Franks.

- Constantinople becomes the capital of the Byzantine Empire.

Apply Social Studies Skills

Using Visuals: **Read a Map**

The map below shows some early civilizations of the Americas. Look at the map, and then answer the questions in your notebook.

▼ The Americas

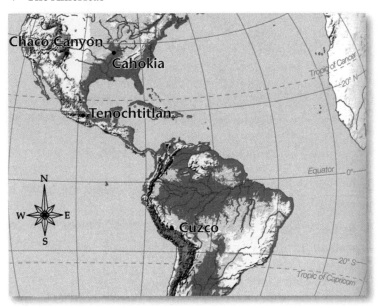

1. Which location is nearest 20°N?

2. Which three locations are north of the equator?

3. Which location is south of the equator?

Extension Project

The Inca civilization was another important early civilization of the Americas. Look online and in reference books to find out where and when the Incas lived. Write a paragraph about the Incas in your notebook.

Read More About It

Look for these books in the library.

▲ Medieval Life
by Andrew Langley

▲ The World of the Medieval Knight
by Christopher Gravett

◀ Japan in the Days of the Samurai
by Virginia Schomp

**For more practice,
go to Workbook pages 61–62.**

Writing Skills

Make an Outline

An outline is one way to help organize the information you are reading about. Look at the model of an outline. Look at the Roman numeral, capital letters, and numbers. See how an outline is shaped.

I.   Main idea
  A.   Detail to support main idea
    1.   supporting information
    2.   supporting information
  B.   Detail to support main idea
    1.   supporting information
    2.   supporting information

Read the following text about the African kingdom of Mali. See how the outline below is created using the information from the text.

The Leaders of Mali

Mali was located in the upper Niger Valley in West Africa. In 1230 its leader, Sundiata, took control of the salt and gold trade from Ghana. Sundiata increased the size of the kingdom.

In 1312 Mansa Musa became the leader of Mali. He also increased the size of the Mali kingdom. He made Islam the official religion of West Africa. Mansa Musa traveled to the holy city of Mecca. He brought the Muslim people of Africa together with the Muslim people of southwest Asia.

I.   The Leaders of Mali
  A.   Sundiata was the leader in 1230.
    1.   He took control of the salt and gold trade.
    2.   He increased the size of the kingdom.
  B.   Mansa Musa was the leader in 1312.
    1.   He increased the size of the kingdom.
    2.   He made Islam the official religion in West Africa.
    3.   He traveled to the holy city of Mecca.

Practice

Read the following information about the history of the East African language Swahili (swah HEE lee). Use the Roman numeral, capital letters, and numbers to make an outline to highlight the important information.

The Swahili Language

During the Middle Ages trade was important between East Africans and Arabs. It led to the development of a new language called Swahili. Swahili was a Bantu (African) language that used some words from the Arabic language. Most people on the trade coast spoke Swahili. Today Swahili is still spoken in Kenya and Tanzania. Most East Africans use Swahili for business.

▼ A Swahili textbook from Tanzania

	0	sifuri		5	tano
	1	moja		6	sita
	2	mbili		7	saba
	3	tatu		8	nane
	4	nne		9	tisa

34   35

For more practice, go to Workbook pages 63–64.

Unit 4

The Renaissance

People

- Francesco Petrarch
- Lorenzo de Medici
- Michelangelo
- Leonardo da Vinci
- Johannes Gutenberg
- Martin Luther
- William Shakespeare
- Prince Henry
- Vasco da Gama
- Christopher Columbus
- Queen Isabella
- Hernán Cortés
- Francisco Pizarro
- Galileo Galilei
- René Descartes
- Isaac Newton

Places

- The Silk Road
- Italy
- Germany
- Portugal
- Spain
- The Americas

Key Events

- The Italian Renaissance
- Invention of the printing press
- The Reformation
- Major voyages of exploration; Columbus sails to the Americas
- Spanish conquests
- The Enlightenment

Get Ready

In your notebook, draw a timeline like the one here. Write an event from Unit 3 for each date.

| 540 | 768 | 1099 | 1100 | 1260 |

Vocabulary

The Roman Catholic Church created a group of **clergy** called Jesuits to help strengthen the Catholic religion in Europe. ▼

▲ Ferdinand Magellan was a Portuguese **explorer**. He sailed to Asia in 1519. He landed in the Philippines in the western Pacific Ocean in 1521.

◄ Martin Luther was a German monk. He made a list of **protests**, or complaints, against the Roman Catholic Church. He put these protests on the door of a church.

Key Words

clergy

explorer

manuscript

movable type

printing press

protests

▲ The **printing press** was an important invention. Before the printing press, a book was a **manuscript** written by hand. The printing press used **movable type**, so the production of a book was much quicker.

Practice

Choose the word that completes each sentence. Write the sentences in your notebook.

1. _____ are public complaints.
   a. Clergy   **b.** Manuscripts   **c.** Protests

2. Magellan visited many new places. He was an _____.
   a. printing press   **b.** explorer   **c.** clergy

3. Leaders of a religion are called _____.
   a. clergy   **b.** movable type   **c.** explorers

4. A machine that printed words on paper was called a _____.
   a. movable type   **b.** printing press   **c.** manuscript

5. A _____ was a book written by hand.
   a. manuscript   **b.** clergy   **c.** printing press

6. _____ improved the way books were made.
   a. Protests   **b.** Manuscripts   **c.** Movable type

For more practice, go to Workbook page 65.

Social Studies Skills

Content Reading Strategy: **Reread**

Good readers use different methods to monitor, or check, their understanding of a text. One method is to **reread**, or read again. Rereading helps you remember more details about the topic or clarify an idea.

Read the following paragraph about an important man in the Renaissance.

Lorenzo de Medici was from a famous and rich family in Florence, Italy. His family owned a bank. Lorenzo and his family paid explorers to discover and bring back things from other parts of the world. Lorenzo loved art, music, and literature. He gave money to many famous artists so that they could paint and write great works.

Now reread the same paragraph with the purpose of understanding who Lorenzo de Medici was and what he did. Did it help you remember the main ideas and some details?

For more practice, go to Workbook pages 66–67.

Using Visuals: **Use Physical Maps**

You have learned some ways that maps can be used. Maps are also used to study the ways that the geography of a country can influence history. The geography of a country influences where, what, and how people live and work. A map that shows the geography of a country is called a physical map.

Look at the physical map of Europe. Look for rivers, mountains, and types of land in the region. Then answer the questions below in your notebook.

▼ Physical map of Europe

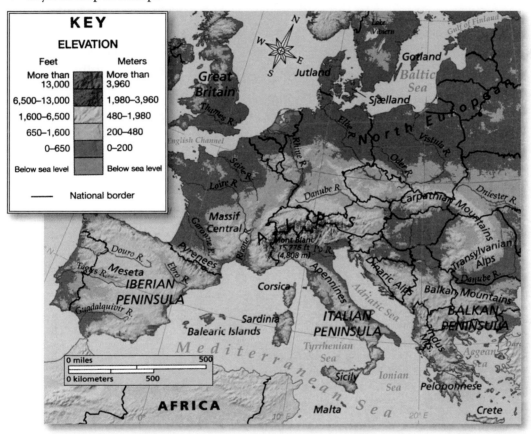

1. What mountain range is on the northern border of the Iberian Peninsula?

2. What is the main river of Great Britain?

3. What is the highest mountain in Europe?

4. What sea is south of Europe?

**For more practice,
go to Workbook page 68.**

Reading ❶

East Meets West

During the Middle Ages there was a series of wars called the Crusades. The Crusaders were Christians from Europe. The Crusaders traveled to the Middle East to take back the city of Jerusalem from the Muslims. Jerusalem was important to Christians for religious reasons. However, Jerusalem was also important to Muslims. The Crusades lasted for 200 years and killed many people. These wars had an interesting and surprising **outcome** for Arab and European cultures. The two groups of people learned about each other.

---

outcome: result

> ### LANGUAGE TIP
> **Phrasal Verbs**
> Some verbs have two or three words. Phrasal verbs cannot be understood by simply putting together the meanings of each word. Look at this list and see how each of these mean different things.
>
> | | |
> |---|---|
> | **take after** | **take in** |
> | **take away** | **take off** |
> | **take back** | **take over** |
> | **take care of** | **take up** |

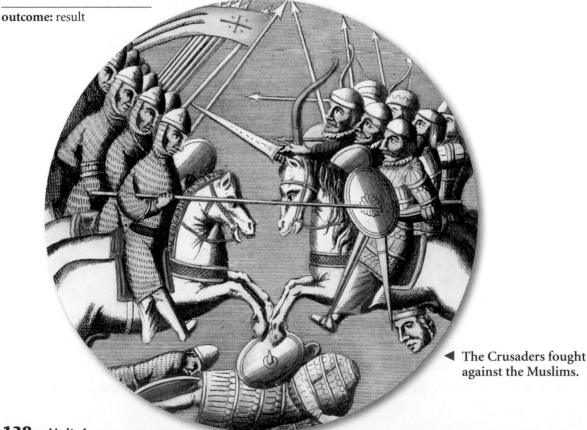

◀ The Crusaders fought against the Muslims.

1209 Scholars leave Oxford
and settle in Cambridge

1302 Flemish workmen
lead revolt against rulers

1321 Dante
Alighieri dies
in Italy

1204 Crusaders
capture Constantinople

1244 Muslims regain
control of Jerusalem

1291 Muslims defeat
Christians at Acre, Egypt

During the Middle Ages, trade grew between Africa, Europe, and Asia. The Italian explorer Marco Polo traveled to Asia. When he returned to Europe, he told people stories about the spices, silk, and other goods that he saw in China. European people wanted these goods. Traders traveled along trade routes called the Silk Road to trade for spices, silk, and rugs from Asia. Trading between countries brought different cultures and languages together.

MORE ABOUT IT

The Silk Road

The Silk Road was a 4,000-mile (6,400-kilometer) trade route from Europe to China. Traders traveled in caravans along this route. From China they brought silk, furs, jade, and ceramics. Few traders traveled the complete route. Most traded with people along the way.

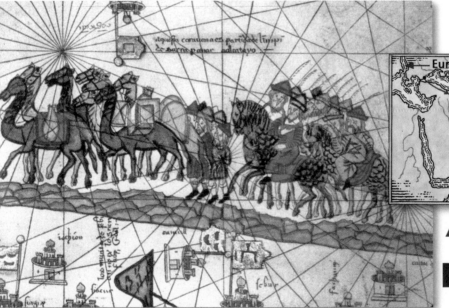

▲ The route of the Silk Road

Before You Go On

1 What were the Crusades?

2. What goods did European traders want from Asia?

3. Why was Marco Polo an important person in history?

| WORLD EVENTS | **1339** Construction begins on Kremlin in Moscow | **1350** Prague becomes capital of Holy Roman Empire | **1385** Portugal becomes independent of Spain |

| UNIT EVENTS | **1341** Petrarch made poet laureate in Rome | | |

Italian Renaissance

The Renaissance was a period of **cultural change** that began in Italy and spread all over Europe. The Renaissance began in the 1300s and continued to the 1600s. The word *renaissance* means **revival** or rebirth. This meant there was a new interest in the ideas, writings, and art of classical Greece and Rome. The Renaissance was a time of great learning, new inventions, beautiful art, and important **literature**. The people who studied the classics were called humanists.

---

cultural change: a change in a society's art, literature, and music
revival: becoming popular again
literature: writing

▼ Italy, 1505

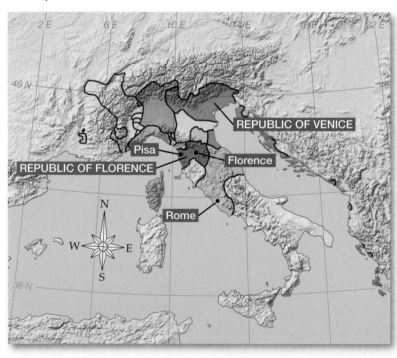

MATH AND ART CONNECTION

Perspective and Proportion

Renaissance artists used two important mathematical ideas in their art: perspective and proportion. Perspective is making faraway objects look realistic. Proportion is the correct relationship between the size and shape of objects. Artists studied texts by the ancient Greeks, who were also interested in these ideas. Below is a perspective line drawing of Leonardo da Vinci's *Last Supper.* (See page 165 for the final painting.)

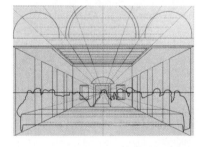

1431 Joan of Arc burned at stake

1433 China outlaws travel to West

1437 Hundred Years' War between France and England ends

1468 Lorenzo de Medici and his brother become rulers of Florence

1492 Lorenzo de Medici dies

1504 Michelangelo creates statue *David*

Francesco Petrarch (1304–1374) was one of the first humanists of the Renaissance. He studied the writings of ancient Rome. He used many of these ideas in his poems about love and nature.

Lorenzo de Medici (1449–1492) was a ruler and **patron** of the arts in Florence, Italy. He was called "Lorenzo the Magnificent." Lorenzo and his family paid explorers to discover and bring back things from other parts of the world. Lorenzo loved art, music, and literature. He supported many famous artists—such as Michelangelo and Leonardo da Vinci—so that they could paint great works.

---

patron: a person who supports someone or something by giving money

▲ *Libyan Sibyl* by Michelangelo. A detail from the ceiling of the Sistine Chapel in Rome.

◀ Florence today

Before You Go On

1. What types of ideas did the humanists study?
2. Who was Lorenzo de Medici?
3. Do you think it is important to support the arts?

The Renaissance **141**

Primary Source

Leonardo da Vinci

Leonardo da Vinci lived during the Renaissance in Italy. He was a painter. But Leonardo was interested in more than just painting. For example, he studied botany. Botany is the science of plants. He studied plants so he could paint flowers and grass better. He also studied sunlight. He saw that sunlight could make shadows or change the color of an object.

Before Leonardo, people's portraits were usually painted as if the people were sitting right in front of the sun. Leonardo did not think this looked right. When he painted, he did experiments with light and shadow. Soon he changed the way people thought about painting.

Below is a passage from one of Leonardo's notebooks. He wrote this in 1480. As you read, look for words you know. They will help you understand the passage.

▲ *La Gioconda*

. . . very great charm of shadow and light is to be found in the faces of those who sit in the doors of dark houses. The eye . . . sees that part of the face which is in shadow lost in the darkness of the house, and that part of the face which is lit draws its [brightness] . . . from the sky. From this light and shade the face gains greatly . . . in beauty . . .

1. How did Leonardo prepare himself to paint flowers?

2. Think about what Leonardo said about the way he wanted to paint a person's face in a portrait. Look at his painting *La Gioconda* (also called *Mona Lisa*). Did Leonardo do what he said he wanted to do?

1503 Michelangelo begins work on Sistine Chapel

1508 Portuguese navy loses battle against Indian and Egyptian navies

1513 Machiavelli writes *The Prince*

1520 Artist Raphael dies in Rome

1522 Martin Luther begins to translate Bible into German

1519 Leonardo dies in France

The Printing Press

An important invention in the Renaissance was the printing press. A German named Johannes Gutenberg invented it. Before the printing press, early books, called manuscripts, were written by hand. It took years to write one manuscript, so books were expensive. Only rich people owned them. The printing press used movable type—the letters could be changed easily. Gutenberg's first printed book was a Bible. The invention of the printing press made it easier and cheaper to make books. More people learned to read. New ideas and **thoughts** were shared everywhere.

---

thoughts: what a person thinks

▼ Gutenberg's workshop

◀ A page from Gutenberg's Bible

CONNECT TO TODAY

Printing

Gutenberg's printing press used metal letters that could be moved around. Later, people developed presses powered with steam called power presses. These presses printed faster. Today we create documents on computers and print with laser printers. Printing is now faster than ever!

Before You Go On

1. What else interested Leonardo besides painting?

2. How were books written before the printing press?

3. What modern invention compares to the printing press? Explain how both inventions changed people's lives.

The Reformation

In the early 1500s Martin Luther, a Roman Catholic monk in Germany, began the Reformation. Luther did not agree with some of the teachings of the Church. For example, the Church taught that people could only go to heaven if they did good **deeds**. Luther believed that **faith** alone was the most important thing. Luther also believed that the Church did some wrong things. He told the Church that it needed to **reform** its ways. He made a list of protests, called 95 theses, and nailed them to a church door.

deeds: acts; things people do
faith: belief in God
reform: change; make better

As You Read

Reread

Why did Martin Luther nail a list of protests to a church door? Reread the paragraph to find more details to help you answer the question.

▼ **Martin Luther and leaders of the Roman Catholic Church**

1544 King Chungjong
of Korea dies

1554 French colony
founded at Rio de Janeiro

1573 Nobunaga
shogunate begins in Japan

1531 German
League formed to
defend Luther

1540 Ignatius Loyola forms
Jesuits to defend Catholic Church
against Protestants

1542 Pope begins Inquisition
in Rome to end Protestantism

The Roman Catholic Church was very angry with Martin Luther. It tried to force German **officials** to punish him. But many people in Germany and other parts of northern Europe agreed with Luther. They joined his **movement**, called Lutheranism. The Lutheran Church became the first Protestant church. **Eventually**, the Roman Catholic Church made some reforms. A group of clergy called Jesuits was created to strengthen the Catholic faith in Europe.

---

officials: people in charge
movement: a group of people who share the same ideas
eventually: after a long time

▼ Major religions in Europe, 1500s

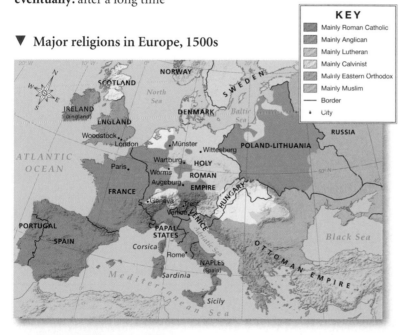

ELSEWHERE IN THE WORLD

William Shakespeare

William Shakespeare (1564–1616) was England's most famous poet and dramatist. He wrote 37 plays. He wrote tragic plays such as *Hamlet* and *Romeo and Juliet,* and comedies such as *A Midsummer Night's Dream.* He also wrote history plays such as *Antony and Cleopatra* and *Julius Caesar.* His plays are still studied and performed today.

Before You Go On

1. Who was Martin Luther?
2. What religions were there in Europe during the 1500s?
3. Why do you think this period is called the Reformation?

Vocabulary

Choose a word from the box to complete each sentence. Write the sentences in your notebook.

manuscript	explorer	clergy
printing press	protests	movable type

1. The _____ meant that many books could be produced quickly.

2. The Jesuits were Roman Catholic _____ .

3. Marco Polo was an _____ who traveled to Asia.

4. Martin Luther nailed his _____ to a church door.

5. Before the printing press, a _____ was written by hand.

6. The printing press made printing easier because it had _____ .

Check Your Understanding

Write the answer to each question in your notebook.

1. Who was Francesco Petrarch?

2. What did Martin Luther do?

3. Name an important invention that was created during the Renaissance.

4. Who were the Jesuits? Why was this group formed?

Apply Social Studies Skills

Content Reading Strategy: **Reread**

Before you read the following paragraph, write down what you remember about the printing press in your notebook. Then read the paragraph. Write down any new details that you remember when you read it again.

> An important invention in the Renaissance was the printing press. A German named Johannes Gutenberg invented it. Before the printing press, early books, called manuscripts, were written by hand. It took years to copy one manuscript, so books were expensive. Only rich people owned them.

Using Visuals: **Use Physical Maps**

Study the physical map of Italy to answer the questions below in your notebook.

▼ Italy, 1510

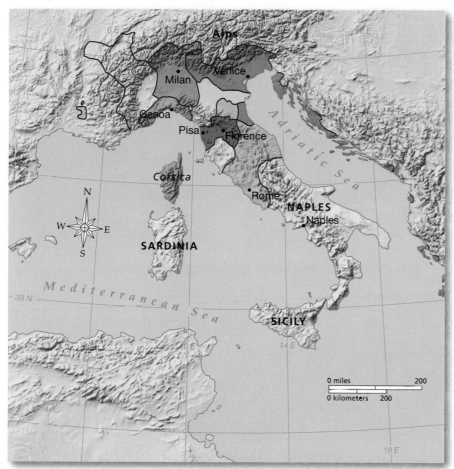

1. How many seas surround Italy? Name them.

2. What mountains are north of Italy?

3. How do you think the shape of Italy might help trade with other countries? Explain your answer.

Discuss

How important is it for people to read about other people's ideas and decide if they are good ideas to follow?

For more practice, go to Workbook pages 69–70.

Vocabulary

◀ The Portuguese made many **voyages** of exploration to other lands.

They used a compass for **navigation**, or to help them find their way. ▼

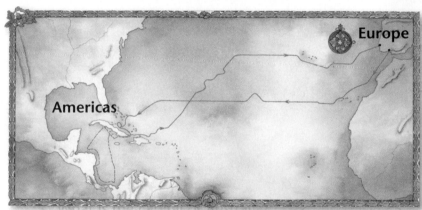

Europe

Americas

◀ This map shows Christopher Columbus's **route** from Europe across the Atlantic Ocean to the Americas, and back to Europe again.

Indigenous peoples such as the Aztecs lived in the Americas. The Europeans **conquered** them and took their land and riches. ▶

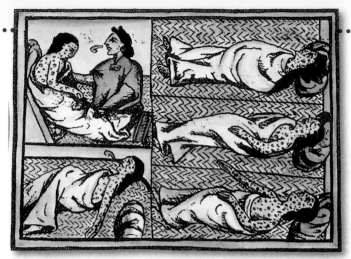

Key Words

conquered

diseases

indigenous

navigation

route

voyages

▲ The Spanish explorers brought many **diseases**, such as smallpox, from Europe. Many indigenous people died from these diseases.

Practice

Choose the word that completes each sentence. Write the sentences in your notebook.

1. _____ are long trips, especially in a ship.
   a. Diseases   **b.** Voyages   **c.** Indigenous

2. An _____ person is original or native to a place.
   a. indigenous   **b.** conquered   **c.** navigation

3. Smallpox was one of the _____ that killed many indigenous people.
   a. voyages   **b.** diseases   **c.** routes

4. When the explorers _____ the indigenous people, they won control.
   a. navigation   **b.** route   **c.** conquered

5. The way from one place to another is called a _____.
   a. disease   **b.** navigation   **c.** route

6. _____ is the science of planning the route of a voyage.
   a. Navigation   **b.** Voyage   **c.** Conquered

For more practice, go to Workbook page 71.

Social Studies Skills

Content Reading Strategy: **Use Selective Attention**

You can **use selective attention** when you read to focus on the information that you need to remember in order to answer a question or write about a topic. It will help you if you find key words and sentences that will answer the question.

For example, think about this question before you read the paragraph below: *What kind of machines did Leonardo da Vinci design?* Look for the answers to the question as you read the paragraph.

Leonardo was an artist, scientist, and inventor. Many of his inventions were machines. He was very interested in flying machines. He studied birds to help him design flying machines. Historians have found drawings for an invention that looks like a helicopter.

Did you find the key words *flying machines* and *helicopter*? If so, you used selective attention to help you to answer the question.

▼ Leonardo's design for a helicopter

For more practice,
go to Workbook pages 72–73.

Using Visuals: **Use Different Types of Maps**

Maps have different purposes. Two types of maps are political maps
and physical maps. A political map shows countries, states, and cities. A
physical map shows mountains, rivers, and plains. It also shows elevation.
Elevation is the height of land above sea level.

Look at the political and physical maps of Portugal and Spain to
answer the questions below. Write the answers in your notebook.

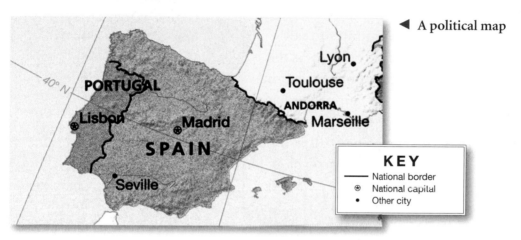

◀ A political map

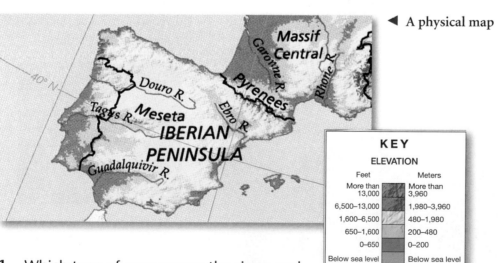

◀ A physical map

1. Which type of map names the rivers and
   mountain ranges?

2. Which type of map names the countries and cities?

3. What are the capitals of Portugal and Spain?

For more practice,
go to Workbook page 74.

Reading ②

Portuguese Exploration

Portugal was the first European country to sail far south on the Atlantic Ocean. Prince Henry was the Portuguese leader. He became an **expert** on navigation. In 1415 he sailed to parts of Africa that Europeans had never been to before. The Portuguese made maps of the areas they explored. Prince Henry used navigation tools that had been invented in China and Arabia to explore the west coast of Africa.

In 1497 a Portuguese explorer named Vasco da Gama sailed around the Cape of Good Hope to India. Before that, people thought it was impossible to sail around Africa.

---

expert: a person with special skill or knowledge

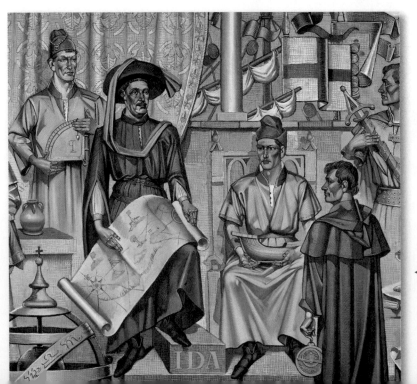

◀ Prince Henry the Navigator and his cartographers (mapmakers)

CONNECT TO TODAY

Maps

In the 1400s the Portuguese made the best maps in Europe. It took a very long time to make a map of a country. The cartographer (mapmaker) created the map as the ship sailed along the coast of a country. The shape was not always correct. Today satellite technology has made mapmaking easy. Computers can make three-dimensional and interactive maps. A Global Positioning System (GPS) in a car is an example of an interactive map.

1461 Muhammad II conquers
last of Byzantine Empire

1477 Vlad the Impaler
dies in Transylvania

1479 King Ferdinand and
Queen Isabella unite Spain

1460
Prince Henry dies

1498 Vasco da Gama
arrives in Calicut, India

Unfortunately, the Portuguese were the first Europeans to bring people from Africa to be sold as **slaves**. In the 1400s slave traders **captured** or bought African people and transported them to Europe. The buying and selling of people from Africa spread to countries on both sides of the Atlantic Ocean. Many enslaved African men, women, and children were sent on long, dangerous trips across the Atlantic Ocean to be sold in the Americas. This slave trade continued for hundreds of years.

slaves: people who are owned by others and are forced to work
captured: took as a prisoner

ELSEWHERE IN THE WORLD

The Kingdom of Mali

The Kingdom of Mali in western Africa was a rich and powerful kingdom. It grew rich from 1200 to 1450 because of the trade in salt and gold. One Mali leader, Mansa Musa, became a Muslim. He extended the kingdom and made Islam the main religion. Mali became a center for learning. Scholars taught mathematics, medicine, law, and religion.

▲ A slave ship

Before You Go On

1. Who was Prince Henry?

2. Where did Vasco da Gama sail?

3. The first word on this page is *unfortunately*. Why do you think this word was used?

Spanish Exploration

An Italian sailor named Christopher Columbus tried to get money from Italy to plan a voyage to India. When Italy **refused** to give him money, Columbus decided to ask Spain for help. The rulers of Spain wanted to sail to India as the Portuguese had done. In 1492 Queen Isabella of Spain gave Columbus money to pay for three ships. Columbus planned to sail west across the Atlantic Ocean. He thought this was the most direct route to India. He did not know that the huge continents of North and South America were in the way. He landed on islands in the Caribbean Sea. He claimed the land for Spain.

---

refused: said no

SCIENCE CONNECTION

Smallpox

Smallpox played a large role in conquering the Aztecs and Incas. The disease made them too sick to fight. Historians believe that before the Europeans arrived, the indigenous population was 20–30 million. By the end of the 16th century, 100 years later, the population was just over 1 million.

◀ Columbus's ships:
Niña, Pinta, and
Santa María

1502 Safavid dynasty
founded in Persia

1503 Pope
Alexander VI dies

1507 German mapmakers
name New World "America"
after explorer Amerigo Vespucci

1500 Columbus returns
to Spain after third voyage

1504 Columbus completes
fourth and last voyage

1506
Columbus dies

People called the Tainos were living on the islands where Columbus landed, in present-day Bahamas. Columbus thought he had landed in India, so he called the Tainos *Indians*. When Columbus returned to Spain, he brought gold, pearls, parrots, and some Taino people, to show to Queen Isabella and King Ferdinand.

The Spanish made the islands a **colony** and the Tainos became slaves. The Spanish brought diseases to the islands. Many Taino people died from these diseases. After 100 years, the Taino people and their culture almost disappeared.

---

colony: a place that is controlled by another country

As You Read

Use Selective Attention

Read question 2 at the bottom of the page. Now read the paragraphs to the left and find the information to answer the question.

Columbus brought some indigenous people to Spain. ▼

Before You Go On

1. Where did Columbus want to go?
2. Who were the Taino people and what happened to them?
3. List two positive things and two negative things about Columbus's voyage.

The Renaissance **155**

WORLD EVENTS

1514 Ottomans crush Persians
at Battle of Chaldiran

1519 Lucrezia Borgia
dies in Italy

UNIT EVENTS

1470 Incas build
Machu Picchu

1519 Hernán Cortés
arrives in Mexico

Spanish Conquests

The Spanish continued to explore. They claimed land all over the Americas for Spain. In 1519 an explorer named Hernán Cortés found a huge city in Mexico called Tenochtitlán. It was the center of the Aztec Empire, ruled by an emperor called Moctezuma. The Aztecs were powerful warriors. They studied the stars and planets, and their **ancestors** had invented an accurate calendar. The Aztecs had never seen white men. They believed that Cortés was a god. However, they soon **realized** that the Spanish were enemies. In 1521 Cortés and his small army destroyed the city.

ancestors: relatives that lived before the present time
realized: found out; became aware

MORE ABOUT IT

Tenochtitlán

Tenochtitlán was built on an island in Lake Texcoco around 1345. The city grew to 200,000 people. Then the Aztecs expanded to the areas around the lake. They connected Tenochtitlán to the mainland by building causeways, long roads above the water. They built floating gardens in the lake. Mexico City was built on top of Tenochtitlán.

▼ Tenochtitlán

1524 Egyptians rebel against Ottoman rule	
	1536 French explorer Jacques Cartier discovers St. Lawrence River in Canada
	1539 Guru Nanak, founder of Sikh movement, dies in India
	1543 Guns first used in Japan

1521 Cortés conquers Aztecs · **1524** Cortés kills last Aztec emperor · **1532** Francisco Pizarro begins travels to Cuzco, Peru · **1533** Pizarro kills Incan emperor

In 1532 another Spanish explorer, Francisco Pizarro, began his travels to Cuzco in Peru. Cuzco was the center of the Inca Empire. In the 1400s the Incan population was 10 million. The Incas built great temples and cities in the mountains. The temples were made of huge stones carved in shapes. The Incas built the city of Machu Picchu in about 1470. They built roads that were hundreds of miles long. The Incas grew **maize**, cocoa, and tobacco on large farms. In 1533 Pizarro arrived in Cuzco. He conquered the Incas and killed their emperor. He stole gold and other **treasures** from the Incan royal family. Incas who were not killed in the conquest died from diseases such as smallpox.

▲ Francisco Pizarro

maize: corn
treasures: things of great value

▼ Machu Picchu

▲ An Incan emperor

Before You Go On

1. Name two cities the Spanish conquered.
2. What did the Incas build?
3. Why do you think the Aztecs thought that Cortés was a god?

| WORLD EVENTS | **1602** Matteo Ricci, an Italian Jesuit, lives in Beijing, China | **1603** James I unites kingdoms of England and Scotland | **1610** Nigerian Queen Amina dies after 34-year rule | **1620** Pilgrims arrive in New England | **1633** Interior of St. Peter's Church in Rome finished |

| UNIT EVENTS | **1619** William Harvey discovers circulation of the blood | **1632** Galileo Galilei publishes *The Dialogue* |

The Enlightenment

During the 1600s scientists began to understand more about the world and how things worked. This period is called the Enlightenment. An Italian scientist called Galileo Galilei was the first person to use a telescope to study the planets and stars. A French philosopher called René Descartes made important discoveries in mathematics. British scientist Robert Boyle discovered the basics of modern chemistry. Isaac Newton studied natural laws and defined the idea of **gravity**. William Harvey figured out how the heart and circulation of the blood works. These people changed how we see the world.

▲ Galileo's telescope

---

gravity: the force that makes things fall to the ground when they are dropped

Profile

Galileo Galilei

Galileo Galilei was born in 1564 in Pisa, Italy. He studied medicine, then mathematics. He taught mathematics at the University of Padua. Around 1604 he began studying astronomy. A new star was discovered that year and he wanted to find out more about it.

In 1609 Galileo heard about the telescope in Venice. A telescope magnifies an object, or makes it seem bigger. The first telescopes magnified objects to three times their real size. In 1610 Galileo made a telescope that magnified objects to thirty times their real size. He sold it to the government in Venice to use as a military tool. Galileo used his telescope to study the sky. He found many new stars and changed people's ideas about the universe.

1649 Charles I of England executed
after losing English Civil War

1637 René Descartes publishes
Discours de la Methode

1661 Robert Boyle publishes
The Sceptical Chymist

1682 Isaac Newton discovers
the law of universal gravitation

Sometimes scientists discovered something that the powerful Roman Catholic Church did not agree with. In 1616 Galileo observed that the earth **revolved** around the sun. At that time, the Church believed the earth was the center of the universe, and that the planets and stars revolved around the earth. For many years Galileo's views annoyed the Church. Galileo was finally brought before the Inquisition, a religious court, in Rome. The court found him guilty. In 1633 Galileo was **sentenced** to stay inside his house for the rest of his life.

revolved: went around
sentenced: punished by a court

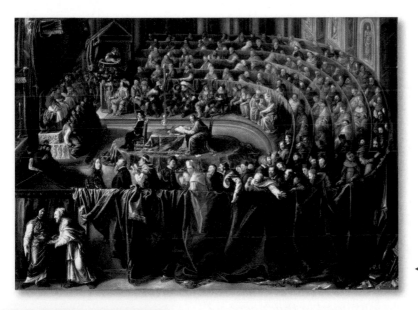

◀ Galileo and the Inquisition

MORE ABOUT IT

The Inquisition

In 1478 an organization called the Inquisition was created by the Roman Catholic Church in Spain. The Inquisition held trials, like court trials, for people accused of non-Catholic beliefs, such as Protestants, Jews, and Muslims. The punishments were horrible. Many people were tortured and burned alive. The Inquisition lasted until the nineteenth century.

Λ neck spiker ▶

Before You Go On

1. Who observed that the earth revolves around the sun?
2. Who discovered the basics of modern chemistry?
3. What do you think a "neck spiker" was used for?

Vocabulary

Choose a word from the box to complete each sentence. Write the sentences in your notebook.

route	conquered	voyages
navigation	diseases	indigenous

1. The Spanish went to Peru and _____ the Incas.

2. Vasco da Gama's _____ was around the Cape of Good Hope.

3. The Spanish explorers sailed on many _____ to the Americas.

4. The Spanish brought _____ that killed many indigenous peoples.

5. The Portuguese made maps to help with _____ .

6. The Aztecs and Incas were the _____ peoples of Mexico and Peru.

Check Your Understanding

Write the answer to each question in your notebook.

1. Name three scientists and their discoveries during the Enlightenment.

2. Who conquered the Aztecs?

3. What did Columbus find on the islands where he landed?

4. Why was Galileo brought before the Inquisition?

Apply Social Studies Skills

Content Reading Strategy: **Use Selective Attention**

Use selective attention while you read the following paragraph to answer the following question: *Who ruled over new Spanish land in the Americas?*

Spain continued to explore and conquer. Spain claimed land all over the Americas. Spain called the different places it claimed viceroyalties. Each viceroyalty was ruled by a viceroy, who was chosen by the leaders in Spain. The Roman Catholic Church and its missionaries helped the viceroys to govern their viceroyalties.

Did the key word *ruled* help you find the answer? Which sentences helped you? Write the answers to the questions in your notebook.

Using Visuals: **Use Different Types of Maps**

Look at the maps to answer the questions below in your notebook.

1. What type of map is the map on the left? The map on the right?
2. What countries are shown on the political map?
3. What features are shown on the physical map?
4. Which map tells you the elevation of Mt. McKinley?

Discuss

The Enlightenment was a period of many discoveries and inventions. Can you think of any inventions today that are changing people's lives? Explain.

For more practice,
go to Workbook pages 75–76.

Unit Review

Vocabulary

Choose a word from the box to complete each sentence. Write the sentences in your notebook.

explorer	manuscript	clergy	conquered
indigenous	voyages	diseases	movable type
protests	printing press	route	navigation

1. Gutenberg invented the _____ so books didn't have to be handwritten.
2. Pizarro killed the Incan emperor and _____ the Incan people.
3. Silk, spices, and rugs came from Asia along a _____ called the Silk Road.
4. The printing press was an important invention because it used _____.
5. Many _____ people died from diseases brought by the explorers.
6. The printing press made it easier to turn a _____ into a book.
7. _____ are religious leaders.
8. Vasco da Gama was a Portuguese _____.
9. Martin Luther posted his _____ on the door of the church.
10. Smallpox is one of the _____ that killed the Aztecs and Incas.
11. The Spanish explorers made many _____ while looking for treasure.
12. Prince Henry was an expert on _____.

Timeline Check

The timeline below has important dates marked on it. Copy the timeline into your notebook and then match the events listed below with the correct date.

1419   1492 1497   1519

- Spanish explorer Hernán Cortés finds the Aztec city of Tenochtitlán
- The Portuguese explorer Vasco da Gama sails around the Cape of Good Hope on his way to India
- Prince Henry sails to parts of Africa that no European had ever been to before
- Queen Isabella of Spain gives Christopher Columbus enough money to buy three ships for a voyage across the Atlantic

Apply Social Studies Skills

Using Visuals: Read a Map

Look at the map key. Then answer the questions below in your notebook.

▲ Central and South America, 1500s

1. What color on the map shows where Portugal had colonies?

2. What color shows where Spain had colonies?

3. Which country had more colonies?

4. How many points are on the compass rose?

Extension Project

Find out what kinds of ships the explorers sailed on in the early 1500s. How big were the ships? What type of power did the ships use? What were they made of? Write the answers in your notebook.

Read More About It

Look for these books in the library.

▲ Christopher Columbus: Famous Explorer by Arlene Bourgeois Molzahn

▲ Renaissance by Alison Cole

◄ The World in the Time of Leonardo da Vinci by Fiona Macdonald

For more practice, go to Workbook pages 77–78.

Writing Skills

Write a First Draft

To write the first draft of a paragraph, it is important to have a well-organized outline.

- Tell yourself what the topic, or main idea, of your paragraph will be.
- Decide what details you want to include.

Now you are ready to write down your facts or ideas as a paragraph.

- Be sure to write in your own words.
- Don't worry about spelling and punctuation in your first draft.
- Write your main idea as your first sentence.

This student has written an outline about South America in the 1500s.

I. Europeans explored South America in the 1400s and 1500s.
   A. South America was claimed by the Portuguese.
      1. Pedro Álvares Cabral landed in Brazil in 1500.
      2. Portugal claimed all of Brazil.
      3. Portugal had no gold or treasures.
   B. Spain was not able to conquer Brazil because of Portugal.

Here is the student's first draft.

European explorers sailed to South America in the 1400s and 1500s. The Portuguese went to brazil before the Spanish had a chance to claim it. An explorerer named cabral landed there in 1500 and he claimed the land for his country Brazil was not like North America because it did not have gold. But at least it was saved from being ruled by spain

Because this is a first draft, it has not been edited yet for correct spelling or punctuation. Right now the student just wants to get her ideas written down as a paragraph.

Practice

Choose a topic to write a paragraph about. Use the information in this unit for your topic. First, write an outline. Then write the first draft of your paragraph. Remember to write in your own words.

Don't worry too much about spelling or punctuation when you write your first draft. You can edit your first draft later.

▼ *The Last Supper* by Leonardo da Vinci

For more practice, go to Workbook pages 79–80.

Unit Contents

People

- Christopher Columbus
- The Pilgrims
- The Puritans
- Native Americans
- The Quakers
- The minutemen
- Thomas Jefferson
- George Washington

Places

- Jamestown
- Plymouth
- Boston
- Philadelphia
- Lexington
- Concord
- Yorktown

Key Events

- Columbus sailed to the Americas
- English settlers formed Jamestown
- The Pilgrims formed Plymouth
- Britain went to war with France
- The Boston Tea Party
- The War for Independence
- The Declaration of Independence
- America became an independent nation
- The Constitution

Get Ready

In your notebook, draw a timeline like the one here. Write an event from Unit 4 for each date.

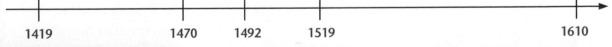

1419   1470 1492 1519   1610

Vocabulary

Jamestown was a **colony**. It belonged to England. English people came to live there. People who make a home, or settle, in a new place are called **settlers**. ▼

▲ An **indentured servant** had to work for four to seven years to gain freedom. Thousands of people came to America as indentured servants.

◄ **Territory** is land that is owned by a government. The British and French governments both wanted American territory.

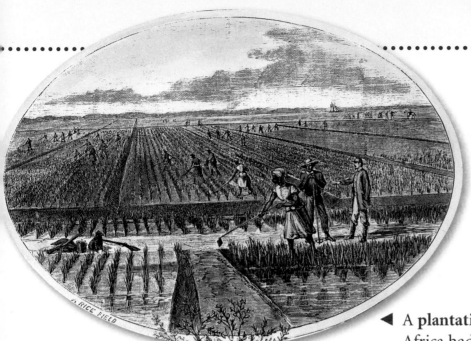

Key Words

colony

indentured servant

plantation

settlers

slaves

territory

◄ A **plantation** is a large farm. **Slaves** from Africa had to work on plantations.

Practice

Choose the word that completes each sentence. Write the sentences in your notebook.

1. People who decide to stay in a new place are called _____.
   a. indentured servants   **b.** settlers   **c.** slaves

2. A _____ was a large farm, usually in the southern colonies.
   a. territory   **b.** colony   **c.** plantation

3. Men and women from Africa who had to work on farms were called _____.
   a. indentured servants   **b.** slaves   **c.** settlers

4. A large area of land is a _____.
   a. territory   **b.** colony   **c.** plantation

5. A _____ is a settled area that belongs to another country.
   a. territory   **b.** plantation   **c.** colony

6. An _____ was a person who had to work for several years to gain freedom.
   a. indentured servant   **b.** settler   **c.** slave

For more practice, go to Workbook page 81.

Social Studies Skills

Content Reading Strategy: **Use What You Know**

To **use what you know** means to think about what you already know about a topic. This helps you understand new information. Ask yourself, "What do I already know that will help me understand what I am reading about?"

For example, you already know what happened to the indigenous people living in the Americas when the Spanish explorers arrived in the New World. Use what you know about this to help you understand what happened to the Native Americans when the English settlers arrived in the Americas.

I know that the Spanish explorers changed the lives of the indigenous people already living there.

The same thing probably happened to the Native Americans when the English came.

Workbook

For more practice, go to Workbook page 82.

Using Visuals: **Read a Chart**

This chart shows things Christopher Columbus took to the Americas. It also shows things he took back to Europe.

Write two things Columbus took to the Americas. Write two things he took to Europe.

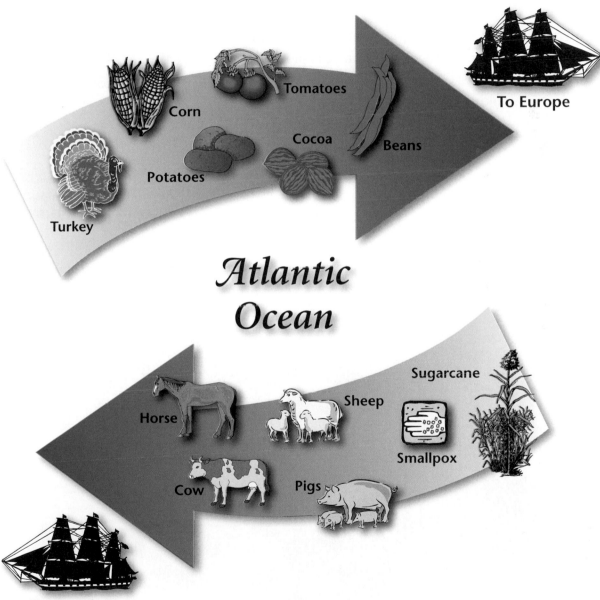

Corn

Tomatoes

Beans

To Europe

Cocoa

Potatoes

Turkey

Atlantic Ocean

Sugarcane

Horse

Sheep

Smallpox

Cow

Pigs

To America

For more practice, go to Workbook pages 83–84.

| WORLD EVENTS | **1301** Ottoman Empire begins | **1325** Aztec Empire begins in Mexico | **1338** Hundred Years' War begins in Europe | **1368** Ming dynasty begins in China |

UNIT EVENTS

Reading ❶

The New World

During the Renaissance, people wanted to learn more about the world. Spain, Portugal, and France explored other lands. Christopher Columbus sailed from Spain in 1492. He was looking for a faster trade route to Asia. He wanted to buy spices, tea, and silk. Usually European traders traveled east to Asia. This took a long time and was very dangerous.

▲ An astrolabe helped sailors navigate using the stars, sun, and moon.

▼ Exploration and navigation increased in the 1500s.

Columbus sailed across the Atlantic Ocean and arrived in the Americas, or the New World. He thought he was near Asia because he didn't know the Americas existed. Columbus claimed the territory for the Spanish. Columbus learned about the people and the land there. After he returned to Europe, he told people what he had learned. His voyages started **contact** between Europe and the Americas.

---

contact: meeting and talking

> ### LANGUAGE TIP
> **Conjunctions**
> A conjunction is a word that joins other words or sentences together. Two conjunctions are *and* and *because*. Look for these words in the paragraph on the left and say which words or sentences they join.

◀ Columbus landed at San Salvador in the modern-day Bahamas.

Before You Go On

1. What was Christopher Columbus looking for?
2. What did Columbus find?
3. Why do you think Columbus believed he was near Asia?

Early United States 173

The English Colonists

English settlers set up colonies in North America in the 1500s and 1600s. These settlers came to America for different reasons. Some people wanted to own land. Other people came for **religious freedom**. These people could not **practice** their religion the way they wanted to in England. Some people came to America as indentured servants. They had to work for a long time to get their freedom.

---

religious freedom: the ability to follow a religion freely
practice: perform; do

MORE ABOUT IT

Indentured Servants

Indentured servants worked without pay for four to seven years. In return, they did not pay for the voyage to America. They received food, clothes, and shelter. The life of indentured servants was very hard. England made some people become indentured servants to punish them. Many people died before they gained their freedom.

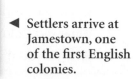

◄ Settlers arrive at Jamestown, one of the first English colonies.

1590
Japan united

1602
Dutch East India
Company founded

1615 *Don Quixote*
published in Spain

1644 Manchu dynasty
begins in China

1587 First English
child born in colonies

1607 Jamestown,
Virginia, settled

1621 First Thanksgiving
celebration

1676 King Philip's Rebellion
between colonists and
Native Americans

The settlers formed the Jamestown colony in Virginia in 1607. They had many problems. Many of the colonists got sick and died during the first winter.

Native Americans lived in North America. They helped the colonists to farm. The colonists used the Native Americans' land and labor. This changed life in North America forever.

Jamestown started its own government in 1619. The government made laws. The colonists had to follow the laws. In the same year, a ship arrived at Jamestown. The ship carried the first slaves from Africa to the colonies.

▲ Many colonists starved during the first winter in Jamestown.

▼ Colonists made bricks to build the first settlement.

An English advertisement for the colony in Virginia ▼

Before You Go On

1. Name two reasons why people came to North America.

2. What happened when they first came to Jamestown?

3. What do you think was most difficult for the new settlers and for the Native Americans?

WORLD EVENTS

UNIT EVENTS

1620 Mayflower lands in Massachusetts

1681 French explore Mississippi River

1692 Salem witch trials

1707 Act of Union unites Great Britain

Pilgrims and Puritans

In 1620 English people called the Pilgrims sailed to the Americas. They wanted religious freedom. Their ship, the *Mayflower*, landed where Massachusetts is today. They called their colony Plymouth.

In 1630 another group of English people, the Puritans, settled in Massachusetts. The Puritans also wanted religious freedom. Puritan leaders made **strict laws**. They did not allow people to practice other religions in their colony.

---

strict laws: laws that had to be carefully obeyed

The Pilgrims sailed to North America on a ship called the *Mayflower*. ▼

CONNECT TO TODAY

Blue Laws

Blue laws stopped people from doing some things on Sundays. The Puritans made the first blue laws. People were not allowed to play card games. People had to go to church. There are still some blue laws today. In some states, selling alcohol in liquor stores on Sundays is against the law. Historians are not sure why the word *blue* is used.

1725 Catherine the Great becomes empress of Russia

1736 Persian Empire invades India

1757 British rule in India begins

1771 James Cook explores Australia

1733 Georgia becomes thirteenth colony

1755 French and Indian War begins

1763 French and Indian War ends

1770 Boston Massacre

The French and Indian War

By 1733 there were thirteen English colonies in North America. France also had colonies there. France and Britain fought a war from 1755 to 1763. Some Native American tribes fought too, some against the French and some against the British. The war was called the French and Indian War. France and Britain both wanted the territory west of the Appalachian Mountains. The French finally surrendered in 1763. They lost a lot of their land in North America.

As You Read

Use What You Know

Have you ever moved to a new country or a new city? Ask yourself: What do I already know that will help me understand the life of the Pilgrims and Puritans?

◀ Some Native Americans fought in the French and Indian War.

Before You Go On

1. Why did the Pilgrims and the Puritans leave England?

2. Why did the French and British fight a war?

3. Would you move to a different country because of your religion? Explain your answer.

Early United States 177

Primary Source

Olaudah Equiano

Olaudah Equiano was the son of an African chief. Slave traders took him to North America. Equiano had a better life than most slaves. He learned to read and write.

In 1789 Equiano wrote a book about his life. Below is a passage from the book. It tells about the slave ship. As you read, look for words you know. They will help you understand the passage.

. . . I became so sick . . . that I was not able to eat, nor had I the least desire to taste anything. I now wished for the last friend, death, to relieve me. . . . In a little time after, amongst the poor chained men, I found some of my own [people], which in a small degree gave ease to my mind. I [asked them] what was to be done with us; they [told] me . . . we were to be carried to these white people's country to work for them.

1. Who are the "poor chained men" that Equiano talks about?

2. What do some of these men tell him?

1707 End of Mughal Empire in India

1755 Lisbon earthquake kills 30,000

1762 Rousseau writes *The Social Contract*

1723 Benjamin Franklin publishes Philadelphia newspaper

1739 Slave revolt in South Carolina

1743 Quakers speak out against slavery

Southern Plantations

The weather was warmer in the southern colonies. The land there was good for farming. The farms were very large. They were called plantations. They grew **tobacco**, rice, and cotton. Plantations needed many workers. Plantation owners bought African slaves to do the work.

Most slaves worked in the fields. Some worked in the houses of the plantation owners. They were servants, cooks, and housekeepers. Other slaves were skilled workers. They were **blacksmiths** or **carpenters**. Most colonists did not think owning slaves was wrong. Some people disagreed. The Quakers wanted to end slavery.

---

tobacco: a plant that people smoke
blacksmiths: people who make things out of iron
carpenters: people who make things out of wood

MORE ABOUT IT

The Quakers
The Quakers were one of the religious groups living in the colonies. They believed in the equality of every human being. They spoke out publicly against slavery as early as 1743. They also spoke out about terrible conditions in prisons and mental hospitals. Quakers helped to settle New Jersey and Pennsylvania.

◀ Slaves picked cotton in the fields.

Before You Go On

1. What did people grow on plantations in the South?
2. Why did the plantation owners buy so many slaves?
3. Compare the lives of slaves and indentured servants.

Vocabulary

Choose a word from the box to complete each sentence. Write the sentences in your notebook.

colony	plantation	indentured servants
slaves	settlers	territory

1. The Pilgrims were _____ in Plymouth Colony.

2. _____ owners bought Africans to work on their farms.

3. France and Britain wanted the _____ west of the Appalachian Mountains.

4. Jamestown was a _____ . People came from England to live there.

5. _____ had to work for several years to pay for their trip to the colonies.

6. _____ worked in the fields and houses of farms in the southern colonies.

Check Your Understanding

Write the answer to each question in your notebook.

1. Why did English settlers come to North America?

2. Where was the first lasting English settlement?

3. Why were African slaves brought to the southern colonies?

4. How did life in North America change for the French after 1763?

Apply Social Studies Skills

Content Reading Strategy: **Use What You Know**

Use what you have learned so far about the British in North America to think about what happened after the French and Indian War. Copy the boxes below into your notebook. Add your ideas to the box on the right.

What I Know	What I Think the British Did Next
• The British wanted to expand their territories. • The French surrendered a lot of their territories in North America.	• •

Using Visuals: **Read a Chart**

This chart shows some of the jobs colonists had. Match the people below with the jobs in the chart. Write the answers in your notebook.

Colonial Jobs			
Jobs in the Colonies	**What They Did**	**Jobs in the Colonies**	**What They Did**
1. Silversmith	Made things out of silver	5. Wheelwright	Made wheels
2. Fisherman	Caught fish	6. Cooper	Made barrels
3. Shoemaker	Made shoes	7. Blacksmith	Made things out of iron
4. Printer	Printed books and newspapers		

I make barrels.

I make things out of iron.

I make wheels.

I make things out of silver.

a.    **b.**    **c.**    **d.**

Discuss

The Puritans came to North America for religious freedom. But in their Massachusetts colony they did not allow anyone to practice a different religion. Do you think this was fair? Why or why not?

Workbook

For more practice, go to Workbook pages 85–86.

Vocabulary

The colonists wanted to be free from Britain. Finally, they agreed to **revolt**, or fight, against England. ▼

▲ These men are **representatives**. They made decisions for other people. They came from the colonies to talk about **independence**.

Destruction of the Tea in Boston Harbor. PAGE 110.

◄ This is the Boston Tea Party. It was a protest against the British **tax** on tea. The tax was extra money the colonists had to pay for tea.

Article 10.

document

independence

representatives

revolt

tax

treaty

◀ A **treaty** is a written agreement, or **document**. Britain and the United States signed the Treaty of Paris in 1783.

Practice

Choose the word that completes each sentence. Write the sentences in your notebook.

1. Something that is formally written is a _____.
   a. tax **b.** revolt **c.** document

2. People who speak for other people in order to make decisions are _____.
   a. representatives **b.** treaty **c.** taxes

3. A _____ is a written agreement between countries.
   a. revolt **b.** tax **c.** treaty

4. When you want to be free, you want _____.
   a. document **b.** independence **c.** tax

5. A _____ is when a group of people fight against control.
   a. treaty **b.** revolt **c.** document

6. A _____ is money people pay to the government.
   a. tax **b.** treaty **c.** independence

For more practice, go to Workbook page 87.

Social Studies Skills

Content Reading Strategy: **Look for Cause and Effect**

Look for causes and effects. Why something happens is a **cause**. What happens is an **effect**. You can also look for words like *because* to help you figure out what is a cause and what is an effect. Here are examples:

Example 1

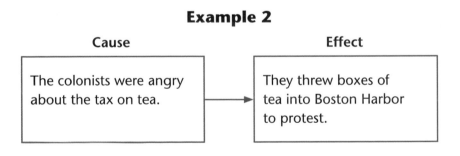

Cause	Effect
The colonists needed people to work on the plantations.	Colonists bought Africans to work as slaves.

The colonists bought Africans to work as slaves *because* they needed people to work on the plantations.

Example 2

Cause	Effect
The colonists were angry about the tax on tea.	They threw boxes of tea into Boston Harbor to protest.

The colonists threw boxes of tea into Boston Harbor *because* they were angry about the tax on tea.

For more practice, go to Workbook pages 88–89.

Using Visuals: **Read a Chart**

Here is a chart about the thirteen colonies. The chart tells you the year each one was founded (started) and when it became a royal colony of the British government. Some colonies were privately owned and not part of the British government. Charts are a good way to look at dates quickly. Read the chart and answer the questions below in your notebook.

The Thirteen Original Colonies		
Colony Name	**Year Founded**	**Year It Became a Royal Colony**
Virginia	1607	1624
Massachusetts	1620	1691
New York	1624	1685
New Hampshire	1629	1679
Maryland	1632	*
Rhode Island	1636	*
Delaware	1638	*
Connecticut	1639	*
North Carolina	1653	1729
New Jersey	1664	1702
South Carolina	1670	1719
Pennsylvania	1681	*
Georgia	1733	1752

* privately owned

1. Which colony was founded first? Which colony was founded last?

2. Which colonies were *not* royal colonies?

3. In what order are the colonies listed? Alphabetical order? Year founded? Year each one became a royal colony?

For more practice, go to Workbook page 90.

Reading ❷

American Independence

The war with France cost Britain a lot of money. The British wanted the colonists to help pay for the war. The British added a tax to many things. These things included **molasses**, newspapers, and tea. The colonists were very angry because they thought the tax laws were unfair. They did not want to **obey** them.

---

molasses: a sweet liquid made from sugar plants
obey: do what someone in authority says to do

As You Read

Look for Cause and Effect

The British wanted the colonists to help pay for the war with France. This caused the British to do something. What was it? What was the effect on the colonists?

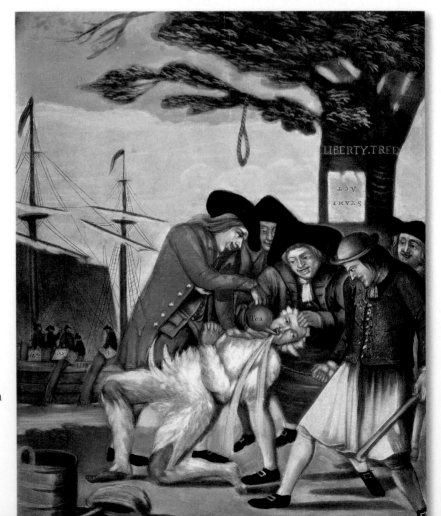

Angry colonists pour tea down the throat of an English tax collector who has been covered in tar and feathers. ▶

186 Unit 5

1762 British capture Caribbean Islands

1772 James Cook goes around Antarctica

1783 First successful hot air balloon

1765 Stamp Act

1769 Daniel Boone crosses the Blue Ridge Mountains

1770 First medical degrees granted in America by Columbia University

1773 Boston Tea Party

The Boston Tea Party

The colonists thought they should have representatives in the British government to speak for them. The colonists decided to **boycott** British goods.

In 1773 a group of colonists in Boston, Massachusetts, dressed up as Native Americans. They climbed onto British ships. The ships had large containers of tea. The colonists threw the tea into the water. This protest was called the Boston Tea Party.

---

boycott: refuse to buy as a protest

MORE ABOUT IT

Tea

China was the first country to use tea. Later, tea became a popular drink all over the world. Europe and America grow very little tea. They must import, or get, it from other countries. The countries that grow the most tea are India, China, and Kenya.

◀ The Boston Tea Party

Before You Go On

1. What things did the British tax?
2. Why did the colonists boycott British goods?
3. What kinds of things do people protest about today?

Early United States **187**

WORLD
EVENTS

1754 First iron mill
opens in England

1759 Britain
captures Québec

UNIT
EVENTS

The British wanted to **punish** the colonists. They closed Boston Harbor. They told the colonists to feed and house British soldiers. The colonists began to think that Britain would never give them freedom. They were becoming **impatient**.

Some colonists thought that the thirteen colonies should be free from Britain. They wanted to become an **independent** country. They decided to act together. Every colony except Georgia sent representatives to Philadelphia. The representatives decided to revolt if the British didn't give them more freedom.

---

punish: hurt people for doing something wrong
impatient: unhappy because something is not happening
independent: free; not ruled by another country

> ### LANGUAGE TIP
> **Past Progressive**
> The past progressive is used to describe a continuous action that happened in the past. It is formed using the past of *to be* + another verb + *-ing*.
>
> I **was**
> You **were**
> He/She **was** } becom**ing** impatient.
> They **were**
> We **were**

◀ A minuteman going to war. The colonists called themselves minutemen because they were ready to fight the British "in a minute."

1762 Britain declares war on Spain   **1764** Russians explore Alaska   **1770** Marie Antoinette marries King Louis XVI of France   **1779** James Cook killed in Hawaii

1775 Paul Revere's ride; start of War for Independence   **1777** Winter at Valley Forge   **1780** Pennsylvania bans slavery; British capture Charleston, South Carolina

The War for Independence

On April 19, 1775, British troops marched from Boston to Lexington and Concord to take the colonists' weapons. The colonists fought back. Nearly 100 colonists were killed or **wounded**. About 250 British soldiers were killed or wounded. This was the beginning of the War for Independence.

wounded: badly hurt

▲ The Battle of Lexington

MORE ABOUT IT

The Musket

The main weapon during this time was a gun called a musket. Muskets didn't shoot very far. It was hard to hit what you were aiming at. Soldiers did not waste time taking aim. Instead, they fired often and reloaded as quickly as they could.

Before You Go On

1. Why did the British punish the colonists?

2. Why did the colonists want to become an independent country?

3. Do you think there is ever a good reason to have a war? Explain.

Early United States   **189**

WORLD
EVENTS

1753 England grants
citizenship to Jews

1760 George III becomes
King of Great Britain

UNIT
EVENTS

1750 Colonial population
exceeds one million

The Declaration of Independence

Soon after the war began, representatives from all thirteen colonies met in Philadelphia again. They voted for independence. Thomas Jefferson wrote a document explaining why the colonists wanted to be independent from Britain. This document is called the Declaration of Independence. It was signed on July 4, 1776. Jefferson's powerful belief in **liberty**, **equality**, and **justice** made many more colonists want to fight against the British.

liberty: freedom
equality: having the same rights as other people
justice: having fair laws

Profile

Thomas Jefferson

Thomas Jefferson was a man of many talents. He was the finest American architect (designer of buildings) of his time. He helped to create the American money system (dollars and cents). He helped to start Virginia's state university. He also played the violin. He later became the third president of the United States.

Collection of the New-York Historical Society

Signing the Declaration of Independence ▶

1769 Napoleon born on Corsica

1774 Québec Act in Canada protects Catholic Church in Canada

1784 First school for the blind opens in Paris

1765 Sons of Liberty attack British governor

1770 Thomas Jefferson calls for freedom of religion

1776 Signing of Declaration of Independence

1780 Benedict Arnold betrays America

1783 Treaty of Paris signed; end of War for Independence

George Washington led the colonial army in many battles during the War for Independence. With the help of the French, Washington **trapped** the British army at Yorktown, Virginia, in 1781. There, the British surrendered. The War for Independence was over.

Britain and the colonies signed the Treaty of Paris in 1783. This treaty made the colonies one independent nation.

---

trapped: put in a place where there is no escape

▼ **The British surrender.**

First School for the Blind

In the late 1700s most people believed that blind people could never learn to read or write. But Valentin Haüy, a Frenchman, studied blind people and watched how they learned things. He wanted to help them. In 1784 Haüy founded the world's first school for the blind in Paris. Louis Braille, who lost his sight when he was four, went to Haüy's school in 1819. At the age of fifteen, he invented the Braille system of writing, using only six dots. This system is still used today.

Before You Go On

1. Name two important people in the fight for independence.
2. What do U.S. citizens celebrate on the Fourth of July?
3. Why do you think the British surrendered?

WORLD EVENTS

1755 *Yankee Doodle* written in England

1760 Dutch explore South Africa

UNIT EVENTS

1754 Colonists and Native Americans sign Albany Plan

1759 First music store opens in America

The United States Constitution

After independence, each colony became a state with its own government. In 1787 the states sent representatives to a meeting in Philadelphia. They wrote a new plan of government. It **united** the states under one government. They called this plan the United States Constitution. It is one of the most important documents in U.S. history.

---

united: joined together

▼ **Signing the United States Constitution**

1768 Gurkhas conquer Nepal

1774 Louis XVI becomes King of France

1782 Bangkok becomes capital of Siam (Thailand)

1771 Spanish missions founded in California

1781 Los Angeles founded

1787 Signing of the U.S. Constitution

1789 George Washington becomes first U.S. president

After the states **approved** the U.S. Constitution, they chose George Washington as the first **president** of the United States. He worked hard to make the new country strong. He was much loved by the people of the United States. One citizen described him as "First in war, first in peace, and first in the hearts of his countrymen."

---

approved: thought something was good
president: elected leader of a country

▲ George Washington

HEALTH CONNECTION

Malaria

George Washington was strong, but he was often ill. One illness he had was malaria. Insects called mosquitoes spread malaria. The illness feels like a very bad flu. People can die from it. Washington did not get treated until he was in his fifties. Luckily for America, he was in good health during the War for Independence.

Before You Go On

1. What was the new plan of government called?

2. What was the main goal of this new plan of government?

3. Do you think it is a good idea to have an army leader become the president? Why or why not?

····Lesson ❷····**Review and Practice**········

Vocabulary

Choose a word from the box to complete each sentence. Write the sentences in your notebook.

document	revolt	tax	independence	representatives	treaty

1. The colonies wanted _____ from Britain.

2. The colonists decided to _____ against the British government.

3. Every colony except Georgia sent _____ to a meeting in Philadelphia.

4. Britain and the colonists signed a _____ after the War for Independence.

5. The British put a _____ on tea and other goods.

6. Thomas Jefferson wrote a _____ explaining why the colonists wanted to be independent from Britain.

Check Your Understanding

Write the answer to each question in your notebook.

1. Why did the British tax the colonists?

2. What decisions did the representatives make in Philadelphia?

3. What is the Declaration of Independence?

4. Why was the United States Constitution important?

Apply Social Studies Skills

Content Reading Strategy: **Look for Cause and Effect**

Copy this chart into your notebook. Fill in the boxes.

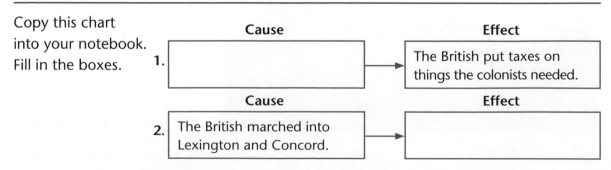

	Cause	Effect
1.		The British put taxes on things the colonists needed.
2.	The British marched into Lexington and Concord.	

Using Visuals: **Read a Chart**

Here is a chart about events that led to the War for Independence. Read the chart. Then answer the questions in your notebook. Remember to think about cause and effect.

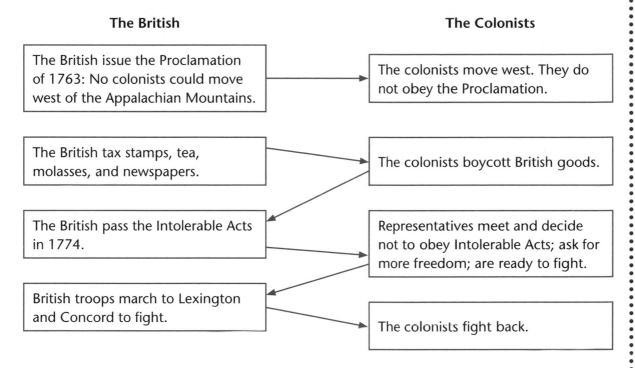

The British   **The Colonists**

The British issue the Proclamation of 1763: No colonists could move west of the Appalachian Mountains. → The colonists move west. They do not obey the Proclamation.

The British tax stamps, tea, molasses, and newspapers. → The colonists boycott British goods.

The British pass the Intolerable Acts in 1774. → Representatives meet and decide not to obey Intolerable Acts; ask for more freedom; are ready to fight.

British troops march to Lexington and Concord to fight. → The colonists fight back.

1. What do the arrows mean?

2. What was the first action that started the conflict between the British and the colonists?

3. According to the chart, what caused the colonists to boycott British goods?

Discuss

The Declaration of Independence says that "all men are created equal." Yet slavery continued for almost another 100 years. Why do you think this happened?

For more practice, go to Workbook pages 91–92.

Unit Review

Vocabulary

Choose a word from the box to complete each sentence. Write the sentences in your notebook.

colony	revolt	settlers	plantation
slaves	tax	Independence	territory
document	Treaty	representatives	indentured servant

1. Christopher Columbus explored new _____.

2. George Washington helped to lead a _____ against Britain.

3. Many English _____ came to America for religious freedom.

4. Plymouth was an English _____ settled by the Pilgrims.

5. A _____ in the South grew mostly tobacco, rice, and cotton.

6. African _____ did most of the work on plantations in the South.

7. Almost every state sent _____ to Philadelphia to talk about the new government.

8. The colonists were angry about the British _____ on tea.

9. To pay for the voyage to North America, an _____ worked for several years.

10. The colonists fought against the British in the War for _____.

11. The U.S. Constitution is an important _____.

12. At the end of the war, the colonists and the British signed the _____ of Paris.

Timeline Check

Put the events in the correct order. Use the timelines in the unit to help you. Write the sentences in your notebook.

_____ France fought with England in the French and Indian War.

_____ Thomas Jefferson wrote the Declaration of Independence.

_____ English settlers formed Jamestown.

_____ The colonists and the British signed the Treaty of Paris.

_____ Christopher Columbus sailed to the Americas.

_____ The Pilgrims sailed from England to Massachusetts.

_____ The colonists threw British tea into the water.

Apply Social Studies Skills

Using Visuals: Read a Chart

This chart shows how France entered the War for Independence. Look at the chart. In your notebook, answer the question: *Why did France help the colonists fight Britain?*

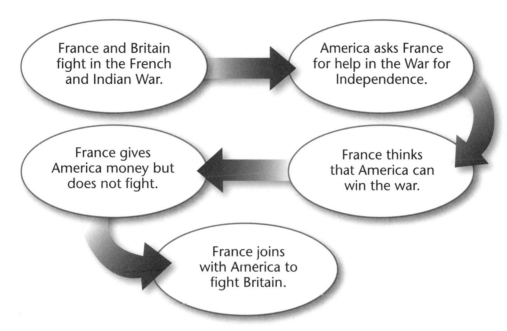

France and Britain fight in the French and Indian War.

America asks France for help in the War for Independence.

France gives America money but does not fight.

France thinks that America can win the war.

France joins with America to fight Britain.

Extension Project

Imagine that you are a colonist. Draw a picture of an event from this time period. Label your picture with words from the unit.

Read More About It

Look for these books in the library.

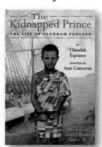

◀ *Give Me Liberty: The Story of the Declaration of Independence* by Russell Freedman

▲ *Stranded at Plimoth Plantation: 1626* by Gary Bowen

▲ *The Kidnapped Prince: The Life of Olaudah Equiano* by Olaudah Equiano, adapted by Ann Cameron

For more practice, go to Workbook pages 93–94.

Writing Skills

Write a Three-Paragraph Essay

Before you write an essay, organize your notes in an outline as you learned to do in Unit 3. Use the outline below to write your essay.

Voyage of the Mayflower

   I. The Pilgrims decided to go to North America.

    A. They wanted religious freedom.

    B. They wanted a new home.

  II. The Voyage of the Mayflower was hard.

    A. The voyage took sixty-five days.

    B. Many people got sick.

 III. The Pilgrims settled where Massachusetts is today.

    A. They named the colony Plymouth.

    B. They made friends with the Native Americans.

    C. They celebrated the end of the first year with a Thanksgiving feast.

Here is a sample of the first paragraph of your essay.

> A group of people called the Pilgrims decided to go to North America from England. They did not have religious freedom in their country. They wanted a new home where they could pray as they wanted.

Practice

Copy the paragraph on page 198 into your notebook. Then write the next two paragraphs of your essay using the outline. Ask yourself the following questions:

- Did I write a topic sentence?

- Is my topic sentence the main idea of the paragraph?

- Did I include a sentence about each detail in the outline?

- Did I use my own words?

For more practice,
go to Workbook pages 95–96.

Unit Contents

People

- George Washington
- John Adams
- Thomas Jefferson
- Meriwether Lewis and William Clark
- Sacagawea and the Shoshone people
- Harriet Tubman
- Frederick Douglass
- Abraham Lincoln
- Ulysses S. Grant
- Robert E. Lee
- John Wilkes Booth
- General George A. Custer
- Chief Joseph

Places

- Missouri River
- Columbia River
- Oregon Trail
- Fort Sumter
- Confederate States of America
- Gettysburg, Pennsylvania
- Ford's Theater, Washington, D.C.
- Little Big Horn, Montana
- Wounded Knee, South Dakota

Key Events

- Westward expansion
- California gold rush
- The Civil War
- Reconstruction
- The reservation system
- The Industrial Age

Get Ready

In your notebook, draw a timeline like the one here. Write an event from Unit 5 for each date.

1584   1607   1770 1776   1787

201

Vocabulary

Pioneers are the first people to go to a new place. In 1848 the discovery of gold in California caused many pioneers to travel west. This period was called the **gold rush**. ▼

▲ A **tribe** is a community of people with a common culture. Many Native American tribes lived on western lands when pioneers from the East arrived.

◄ An **immigrant** is a person who moves to a new country to live and work. Immigrants from China and Ireland worked on the railroads.

◄ A **wagon train** was a group of covered wagons. Pioneers traveled in wagon trains across the Great Plains of North America.

Key Words

gold rush

immigrant

industry

pioneers

tribe

wagon train

▲ The business of making things is called **industry**.
In the 1800s the North had many factories and
cities. Factories are a large part of industry.

Practice

Choose the word that completes each sentence. Write the sentences in
your notebook.

1. When people went to California to find gold it was called the _____.
   a. gold rush   **b.** pioneers   **c.** industry

2. Groups of Native Americans with a common culture are _____.
   a. immigrants   **b.** pioneers   **c.** tribes

3. _____ are people who move to a different country to work and live.
   a. Wagon trains   **b.** Immigrants   **c.** Tribes

4. _____ were the people that moved west across the Great Plains.
   a. Pioneers   **b.** Wagon trains   **c.** Immigrants

5. A group of covered wagons is a _____.
   a. industry   **b.** wagon train   **c.** gold rush

6. Making things in factories is called _____.
   a. tribes   **b.** immigrants   **c.** industry

For more practice, go to Workbook page 97.

Social Studies Skills

Content Reading Strategy: **Compare and Contrast**

To **compare and contrast** means to think about how two things are the same (compare) and how they are different (contrast). A Venn diagram can help organize your thinking. Read the following sentences and look at the diagram below.

In the 1800s there were two kinds of workers in the United States. Slaves were the property of their owners. Hired workers were paid for their work.

Slaves	**Both**	**Hired Workers**
got food, clothes, and housing from their master	needed food, clothing, and housing	got their own food, clothing, and housing
did not get money for work	worked hard	got money for doing work
could not leave	worked all day	could move from place to place
could not quit their jobs	worked at different kinds of jobs	could quit their jobs

The things listed under the headings "Slaves" and "Hired Workers" are the ways their lives were different. The things listed under the heading "Both" are the ways their lives were the same.

**For more practice,
go to Workbook pages 98–99.**

Using Visuals: **Read a Graph**

A graph is a way to organize information using numbers. Circle graphs (sometimes called pie charts) are often used to show percents. The whole circle graph equals 100 percent. Use the circle graph to answer the questions below in your notebook.

Colonial Population, 1775: Countries of Origin

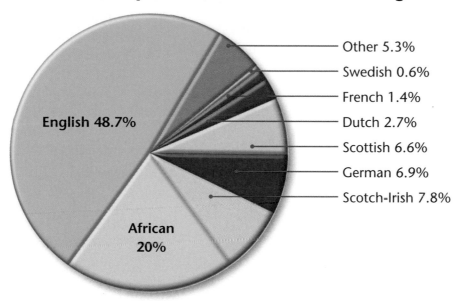

1. What country had the most colonists in 1775?

2. What country had the second most colonists in 1775?

3. Compare the reasons these two groups had for being in the colonies in 1775.

For more practice, go to Workbook page 100.

Reading ❶

The First Presidency

After the War for Independence, the colonists formed a new nation. In 1789 George Washington became the first president of the United States. The new government made a Constitution. Ten amendments were soon approved and added to the Constitution. These amendments are called the Bill of Rights. The Bill of Rights is important because it tells people that they have certain rights that no one can take away. For example, it says that there are rules to protect people if they are **accused** of a crime. People also have freedom of religion, speech, and **assembly**.

---

accused: said to have done something wrong
assembly: meeting of a group of people

ELSEWHERE IN THE WORLD

The Haitian Revolution

In 1791 Toussaint L'Ouverture, a former slave, started a revolution in the French colony called Saint-Domingue in the Caribbean Sea. He defeated Spanish and British armies who wanted this rich colony. In 1804 Saint-Domingue was declared an independent nation. The leaders named the new nation Haiti. Haiti became the first independent nation in Latin America.

▲ The United States Constitution

1796 Imperial Chinese government forbids import of opium to China

1799 Rosetta Stone found in Egypt; hieroglyphics decoded

1804 Napoleon Bonaparte becomes emperor of France

1797 John Adams becomes second president of U.S.

1798 U.S. Marine Corps created

1799 George Washington dies in Virginia

As the first president, George Washington had many **challenges**. He had to build the nation's first government, pay off a national **debt** from war, and establish a bank of the United States. His vice-president was John Adams. Washington had a group of advisers to help him. These men were called his cabinet. Washington was president for eight years and retired in 1797. John Adams was the next president.

---

challenges: things that are difficult for someone
debt: money owed to someone

MORE ABOUT IT

First U.S. Coin

The first U.S. coins were produced in 1787 in Connecticut. The coin was a large one-cent piece. One side of the coin showed a chain with thirteen links. The chain symbolized the thirteen colonies. Many people were unhappy with the chain symbol. It was later replaced.

◄ George Washington, his wife, Martha, and their children

Before You Go On

1. How many years did George Washington serve as president?

2. What are the first ten amendments called?

3. Why do you think some people did not like the image of chains on the first U.S. coin?

WORLD EVENTS

1805 Modern nation of Egypt established by Pasha Mehemet Ali

1810 Mexico wins its independence from Spain

1815 Napoleon defeated at Waterloo

UNIT EVENTS

1803 United States buys Louisiana territory from France

1804 Lewis and Clark's expedition begins

1810 Former slave Tom Molineaux becomes first American boxer to fight for a world title

1814 Francis Scott Key writes *Star Spangled Banner*

Settlers and Explorers

As You Read

Compare and Contrast

Use what you know to compare and contrast what Lewis and Clark found in the new territories to what they were used to. Make a Venn diagram like the one on page 204 to help you.

After the new nation was formed, some settlers moved west to find land to farm and claim as their own. Settlers who moved west to explore new territories were called pioneers. In 1804 President Thomas Jefferson sent two men, Meriwether Lewis and William Clark, to explore the territory west of the Mississippi River. A group of men went with them. They set out from St. Louis and traveled on the Missouri River. President Jefferson hoped they would find a water route across the **continent** to the Pacific Ocean.

continent: a large area of land

▼ The route of Lewis and Clark's expedition

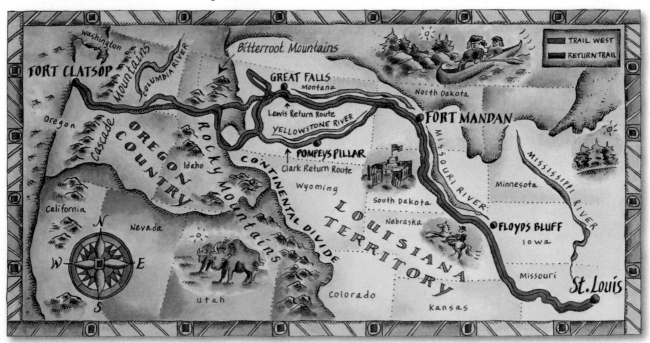

| 1826 First railroad tunnel completed in England | | 1833 Abolition of slavery in British Empire | 1837 Victoria becomes Queen of England; rules until 1901 |

1820 The Missouri Compromise tries to balance slave states and free states

1830 Mormons, or the Church of Jesus Christ of Latter-Day Saints, founded by Joseph Smith

1836 American settlers defeated by Mexican Army at Alamo

The Missouri River ended in the Rocky Mountains. There was no river that ran west from the Rocky Mountains to the Pacific Ocean. They had to walk to keep going west. They met many Native American tribes along the way. A Shoshone woman, Sacagawea, and her baby, Jean Baptiste, traveled with them as their guide and translator. The Shoshone people gave Lewis and Clark horses to cross the Rocky Mountains. Finally, they got to the Columbia River, which led them to the Pacific Ocean.

▲ Lewis and Clark on the Columbia River

MORE ABOUT IT

The Shoshone People

Lewis and Clark met the Shoshone people and received their help. The Shoshone were a nomadic people who carried few belongings and moved from place to place. When they got horses sometime in the 1700s, it changed their lifestyle. They could travel further and hunt larger animals. They traveled all over the western United States until the settlers took the land.

Before You Go On

1. What did President Jefferson want Lewis and Clark to find?

2. Who went with them to help them talk with the tribes they would meet?

3. Lewis and Clark could not take enough food for their trip. What do you think they ate as they traveled?

Westward Movement

In the 1840s thousands of pioneers traveled west along a route called the Oregon Trail. They traveled in wagon trains.

In 1848 gold was discovered near San Francisco. After the discovery, more people traveled to the West. They hoped to find gold and get rich. This was called the gold rush.

At first, life was very hard in the West. There was sickness, hard work, and **isolation**. People kept in touch by sending **mail** through the Pony Express.

---

isolation: being away from other people and things
mail: letters and packages sent from one place to another

▼ By 1870 more than 300,000 people had traveled west by wagon train.

MORE ABOUT IT

The Pony Express
The Pony Express carried mail west from Missouri to California. A rider with a bag of mail rode a horse very fast for about ten miles. Then the mail was given to the next rider. Most of the riders were young men, even teenagers. The Pony Express helped settlers in the West feel connected to the East. The Pony Express ended in 1861, after the telegraph was invented. A telegraph message could be sent over wires quickly.

PONY EXPRESS
St. JOSEPH, MISSOURI to CALIFORNIA
in 10 days or less.

☞ **WANTED** ☜

YOUNG, SKINNY, WIRY FELLOWS
not over eighteen. Must be expert riders, willing to risk death daily.
Orphans preferred.
Wages $25 per week.

APPLY, **PONY EXPRESS STABLES**
St. JOSEPH, MISSOURI

1844 Young Men's Christian Association (YMCA) founded in England

1847 Liberia becomes an independent republic in Africa

1848 First settlers arrive in New Zealand

1850 Taiping Rebellion against Ching dynasty in China

1844 Samuel F. Morse sends first telegram

1847 Mexican-American War ends; Mexico forced to give up much of its northern territory

1848 Gold rush begins in California

1851 *New York Times* first published

Buffalo had lived in North America for thousands of years. The Europeans brought **cattle** to North America. Cowboys moved some of the cattle across the plains. Buffalo and cattle both eat grass. The cattle in the West took over land that was used by the buffalo for food. Many buffalo died. Native Americans also hunted them for food and to make clothes from their skins.

In the 1860s the government **funded** two **transcontinental** railroads—the Union Pacific and the Central Pacific. It took seven years to build these railroads. Many Irish and Chinese immigrants worked on the railroads. The work was difficult and dangerous.

---

cattle: groups of cows
funded: gave money to make something happen
transcontinental: crossing a continent

CONNECT TO
TODAY

Railroad Travel

Today, railroads are a very important way of travel for passengers and goods. Long lines of freight cars carry oil, grain, fruit, vegetables, and many other products all over the country. There are about 150,000 miles (240,000 kilometers) of railroad track in the United States.

Before You Go On

1. Where were the pioneers going? Why?
2. Why did the buffalo die?
3. Why do you think the government wanted to build a railroad across the United States?

▲ A cowboy and his cattle

WORLD EVENTS				**1852** Napoleon III becomes emperor of France	**1854** Crimean War begins

| UNIT EVENTS | **1850** Compromise of 1850 tries to settle the slavery debate | **1851** Clipper ship *Flying Cloud* sets record for fastest voyage from New York to San Francisco | **1852** Harriet Beecher Stowe's *Uncle Tom's Cabin* is published | **1854** Horace Smith and Daniel Wesson develop Smith and Wesson revolver (gun) |

The Abolitionists

By the early 1850s the people who lived in the North did not agree with the people who lived in the South. Many people in the North worked in industry and were paid for their work. Many Northerners wanted to **abolish** slavery because it was cruel and because the Constitution said people had the right to be free. The abolitionists **spoke out** against slavery. People in the South did not want to stop slavery because they used the slaves to pick cotton and work in the fields. Southerners did not want to change their way of life.

---

abolish: stop; get rid of
spoke out: protested

Profile

Harriet Tubman

Harriet Tubman was born a slave in Bucktown, Maryland, around 1820. When she was seven years old, she was sold to another owner, who beat her. In 1844 Harriet met and married John Tubman, a free man. Five years later, Harriet ran away to freedom on the Underground Railroad. The Underground Railroad was a series of places where a runaway could stay and be safe. But Harriet did not forget her life as a slave. She went back to the South nineteen times to help other slaves escape. Harriet freed 300 slaves before the Civil War. Then, from 1862 to 1864, she was a spy for the Union army.

In 1908 Harriet bought a house in Auburn, New York. She worked for the poor. Harriet Tubman died of pneumonia at her home on March 10, 1913. She was about ninety-three years old.

1855 Austrian engineer Franz
Koller develops tungsten steel

1858 India becomes
part of British Empire

1860 Ettiene Lenoir constructs
first internal combustion engine

1857
Dred Scott decision

1859 World's first
oil well dug in Titusville,
Pennsylvania

Frederick Douglass was an African-American abolitionist. He was born into slavery in Maryland. Douglass **defied** the rules by learning to read. In 1838 he escaped to the North. He spoke at antislavery meetings across the United States. He **published** an antislavery newspaper.

By 1860 the nation had become more and more divided. Some states were slave states and some states were free states.

---

defied: refused to obey
published: printed and sold to the public

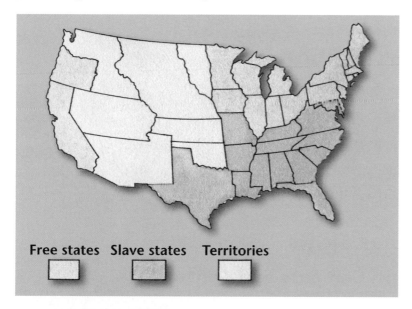

Free states   Slave states   Territories

▲ Free states and slave states

Before You Go On

1. Who was Frederick Douglass?
2. What was a free state? A slave state?
3. Describe a rule, a law, or an issue of today that you do not agree with. Explain why.

SCIENCE CONNECTION

Environmental Science

Industry in the North created many jobs. It also caused a lot of pollution such as smog. Smog is a mixture of smoke and fog. It is created by the smoke of burning coal from factories or car fumes. In London in the winter of 1952, 12,000 people died as a result of smog. Heavy fog mixed with coal-burning fumes made the air toxic. This disaster was the start of the modern environmentalist movement. Today in the United States, the burning of coal is more controlled than in the past.

A New Nation   213

Vocabulary

Choose a word from the box to complete each sentence. Write the sentences in your notebook.

industry	gold rush	pioneers
tribe	wagon train	immigrant

1. The _____ traveled across the Rocky Mountains to settle new lands.

2. Lewis and Clark met a Native American _____ called the Shoshone.

3. In the _____ of 1848, many people went to California to look for gold.

4. Making products in factories was the _____ of the North.

5. A person who moves to a new country to live and work is an _____.

6. A group of pioneers traveled together in a _____ .

Check Your Understanding

Write the answer to each question in your notebook.

1. What did Lewis and Clark do?

2. Why did many people move to the West?

3. Why didn't the people of the North and South agree?

4. Who was Harriet Tubman?

Apply Social Studies Skills

Content Reading Strategy: **Compare and Contrast**

Compare Harriet Tubman to Frederick Douglass. Create a Venn diagram in your notebook like the one on page 204. Use the diagram to compare and contrast the two people.

Using Visuals: **Read a Graph**

Look at the circle graph about slavery.
Then answer the questions below in your notebook.

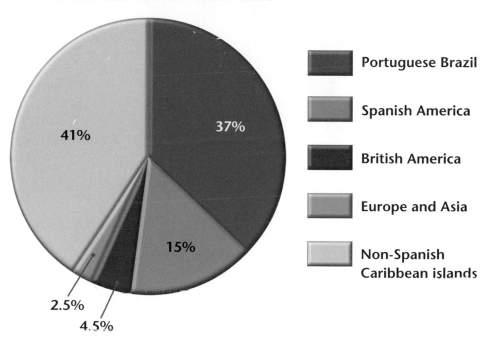

Where the Slaves Were Sent

- Portuguese Brazil
- Spanish America
- British America
- Europe and Asia
- Non-Spanish Caribbean islands

37%
41%
15%
2.5%
4.5%

1. What percentage of slaves went to British America?
2. What percentage of slaves went to Portuguese Brazil?
3. Which of the Americas received the largest number of African slaves, North America or South America?

Discuss

The pioneers faced many hardships and dangers when they traveled west.
Compare traveling west today to traveling during the time of wagon trains.

For more practice, go to Workbook pages 101–102.

Vocabulary

◄ Before the Civil War, the United States was under one government in Washington, D.C. But the southern and northern states divided. The South was called the **Confederacy**. The North was called the **Union**. The line between the northern and southern states was called the **Mason-Dixon Line**.

A **fort** is a group of buildings surrounded by walls and fences to defend people from danger. Soldiers can live in a fort. ►

◄ A **battle** was fought at Fort Sumter and the Civil War began. A battle is a fight between two groups of soldiers. During the Civil War, there were many battles between the Confederacy and the Union.

Key Words

battle

Confederacy

fort

Mason-Dixon Line

railroads

Union

▲ **Railroads,** or the tracks that trains use, provided transportation for people and goods. By 1860 immigrants had built more than 30,000 miles of railroads.

Practice

Choose the word that completes each sentence. Write the sentences in your notebook.

1. During the Civil War, northern states were called the _____.
   a. Mason-Dixon Line   **b.** Union   **c.** Confederacy

2. Southern states were called the _____.
   a. Confederacy   **b.** battle   **c.** Union

3. The _____ was an imaginary division that separated the North and South.
   a. Union   **b.** Mason-Dixon Line   **c.** fort

4. A fight between two groups of soldiers is a _____.
   a. fort   **b.** expansion   **c.** battle

5. A _____ is a place built to protect people.
   a. Union   **b.** Mason-Dixon Line   **c.** fort

6. The _____ transported people and goods around the United States.
   a. railroads   **b.** Confederacy   **c.** Union

For more practice, go to Workbook page 103.

Social Studies Skills

Content Reading Strategy: **Draw Conclusions**

When you **draw a conclusion** you add up the details in the information that you have just read. You put together the clues in the text and use what you already know.

Read the paragraph and look at the graphic organizer.

Harriet Beecher Stowe wrote *Uncle Tom's Cabin*. This book showed how terrible slavery was. The book caused a lot of northerners to want to stop slavery in the United States. This made southern plantation owners angry. They did not want to lose their slaves. They did not want to change their way of life.

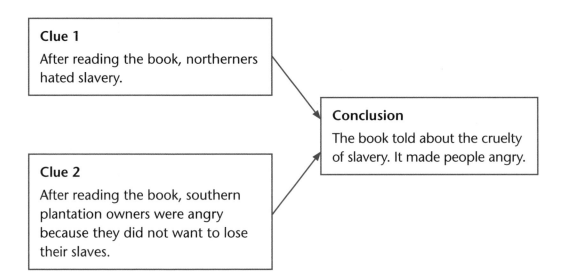

Clue 1
After reading the book, northerners hated slavery.

Clue 2
After reading the book, southern plantation owners were angry because they did not want to lose their slaves.

Conclusion
The book told about the cruelty of slavery. It made people angry.

From the reaction of northerners and southerners, you can draw the conclusion that the book *Uncle Tom's Cabin* showed the cruelty of slavery. It made northerners angry about slavery, and southerners angry with northerners because they did not want to change their way of life.

For more practice, go to Workbook pages 104–105.

Using Visuals: **Read a Graph**

A bar graph shows numbers of things. You can measure one bar against another to compare things.

- Look at the titles and ask yourself what each graph is about.
- Read the labels on the left of each graph.
- Look at the numbers on the bottom of each graph.
- Draw conclusions about what each graph tells you.

Use the bar graphs below to answer the questions in your notebook.

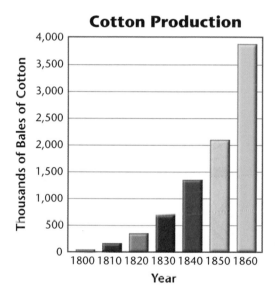

1. How many slaves were there in 1800? How many slaves were there by 1860?

2. Draw a conclusion about slavery and the bales of cotton grown using the data on the graphs. Which of these two conclusions do you agree with? Explain your choice.

   - The number of bales of cotton grown depended on how many slaves there were.

       or

   - There is no connection between how much cotton was grown and how many slaves there were.

For more practice,
go to Workbook page 106.

WORLD
EVENTS

1862 Bismarck becomes
Prussian prime minister

1863 Archduke Maximilian of Austria
proclaimed emperor of Mexico

UNIT
EVENTS

1861
Civil War begins

1863 Abraham Lincoln signs
Emancipation Proclamation

Reading ❷

The Civil War

Abraham Lincoln became president in 1860. The South did not like Lincoln's views. By early 1861 most of the southern states below the Mason-Dixon Line had **seceded**. They wanted to be a separate country called the Confederate States of America, or the Confederacy. They fought to be able to govern themselves. The Civil War began with a battle at Fort Sumter in South Carolina on April 12, 1861.

The Union won an important battle at Gettysburg in Pennsylvania. More than 50,000 men died or were wounded. President Lincoln later gave a speech, the Gettysburg Address, to honor the men who died there.

---

seceded: left; withdrew from

▲ Lincoln at Gettysburg

As You Read

Draw Conclusions

Think about the different groups of people living in the United States during the 1800s. Draw a conclusion about how each group felt.

MUSIC
CONNECTION

Songs of the Civil War

Singing was a very popular activity for the soldiers. There were some songs that had two versions because both sides, Union and Confederate, sang them. Many of the Civil War songs survive today. For example, "When Johnny Comes Marching Home" is still very well known.

1866 Alfred Nobel invents dynamite

1868 Shogunate abolished in Japan

1869 Suez Canal in Egypt opens

1865 Civil War ends; President Lincoln assassinated

1867 United States purchases Alaska from Russia

1868 Civil War general Ulysses S. Grant elected president of the United States

The war lasted four years. In 1864 President Lincoln made General Ulysses S. Grant the commander-in-chief of the Union army. General Robert E. Lee was the commander-in-chief of the Confederate army. The Union won many battles under Grant's leadership. On April 9, 1865, General Lee surrendered. The Civil War ended.

Much of the South had been **destroyed** by the war. President Lincoln wanted to help the South **rejoin** the Union, but he did not live to see it happen. On April 14, 1865, John Wilkes Booth **assassinated** the president while he was watching a play at Ford's Theater in Washington, D.C. Booth was a supporter of the Confederacy.

---

destroyed: ruined completely
rejoin: come back
assassinated: killed for political reasons

▲ Much of the South was destroyed.

MORE ABOUT IT

Women in the Civil War

Thousands of nurses, as well as 400 other women, served in the Civil War on both sides. Dr. Mary Walker, one of the earliest female surgeons, won the Medal of Honor for her work during the Civil War. Susie Baker, a former slave, taught soldiers to read and write when she was only fourteen.

Dr. Mary Walker
Army Surgeon

Medal of Honor
USA 20c

Before You Go On

1. What did the southern states call themselves?

2. Why did President Lincoln give the Gettysburg Address?

3. Do you know of any civil wars (wars between different groups in the same country) in more recent times?

Reconstruction

The period from 1865 to 1877 is called the Reconstruction period. The government's plan was to reconstruct, or rebuild, the United States. The eleven southern states that had seceded had to be brought back into the Union.

It was a difficult task. Southern leaders passed laws to stop African Americans from voting and working. They wanted to keep African Americans **segregated**. Congress passed amendments to the Constitution to help African Americans. The Fourteenth Amendment said that states could not **deny** rights to United States citizens. The Fifteenth Amendment said that all men had the right to vote. Reconstruction of the South ended in 1877.

segregated: separated because of race or class
deny: stop from having

Civil Rights Movement

Many southerners did not want African Americans to have the right to vote. Organizations such as the Ku Klux Klan tried to stop them through fear and violence. Southern states made it difficult in other ways for African Americans to vote.

The American Civil Rights movement, led by Dr. Martin Luther King Jr., aimed to give African Americans the same rights as whites. The movement organized marches, boycotts, and protests. Finally, Congress passed the *Voting Rights Act* of 1965, allowing African Americans to vote freely.

◄ African-American men vote in 1868, after the Fourteenth Amendment was passed.

1874 First exhibit of Impressionist paintings in Paris

1876 Korea becomes an independent nation

1877 Queen Victoria becomes empress of India

1879 Zulu nation fights British in Africa

1873 Remington & Sons produce first typewriters

1874 Apache chief Cochise dies of natural causes

1876 Battle of Little Big Horn

1877 Reconstruction ends

The Reservation System

By the 1860s the United States government wanted to expand. It wanted more territory. It decided that Native Americans had to live on **reservations**. They could not travel freely anymore. Farmers and ranchers fenced in the cattle and shot the buffalo.

In 1876 leaders from the Sioux and Cheyenne tribes refused to move to a reservation. The United States government sent General George A. Custer to fight the Native Americans. The battle took place at Little Big Horn in Montana. General Custer and all his men were killed. The Native Americans won this battle, but not the larger fight to keep their lands.

---

reservations: areas of land specifically for Native Americans

▲ The Battle of Little Big Horn

MORE ABOUT IT

Indian Boarding Schools

From 1870 many Native American children were sent to "Indian boarding schools." By 1900 there were 17,000 children in 153 schools. The children had to learn to speak, dress, and act like white children. They had to forget their own language, religion, and culture.

Before You Go On

1. What happened during the Reconstruction period?

2. What is a reservation?

3. What do people protest about today?

WORLD EVENTS

1879 War of the Pacific begins

1881 First political parties founded in Japan

UNIT EVENTS

1877 U.S. soldiers attack Chief Joseph and his tribe

1881 President James Garfield assassinated

1882 United States outlaws Chinese immigration for ten-year period

Primary Source

Chief Joseph

Chief Joseph's father made a treaty with the U.S. government in 1855. That treaty said the Nez Percé tribe could stay on their land in the northwestern territory (Idaho–Washington). In 1863 the government wanted to make a different treaty to reduce the amount of land. Old Joseph died and young Chief Joseph (1840–1904) led the fight against the federal soldiers. After much fighting, Chief Joseph and his tribe surrendered. Chief Joseph visited the president in Washington, D.C., to try to change his mind. Several years later, most of the Nez Percé were allowed to go back to the Pacific Northwest. There were not many other tribe members remaining by then.

Below is a passage from one of Chief Joseph's many speeches against injustice. As you read, look for words you know. They will help you understand the passage.

The first white men of your people who came to our country were named Lewis and Clark. . . . They made presents to our chiefs and our people made presents to them. . . . All the Nez Percé made friends with Lewis and Clark and agreed to let them pass through their country and never to make war on the white men. This promise the Nez Percé have never broken.

1. What did Lewis and Clark exchange with the Nez Percé?

2. What promise did Chief Joseph say the Nez Percé had never broken?

1883 *Orient Express* train makes first run from Paris to Istanbul

1884 Berlin Conference held to discuss European division of colonial Africa

1885 Congo becomes the personal possession of King Leopold of Belgium

1886 First Indian National Congress meets

1886 Haymarket labor rally in Chicago ends in violence

1890 Sitting Bull shot and killed; Battle of Wounded Knee takes place

In 1877 U.S. soldiers attacked the Nez Percé tribe. Chief Joseph and his tribe fought back. They fled to Canada. The soldiers followed them for two months. Finally, the soldiers **captured** the tribe. Many people had died from cold and **starvation**.

In 1890 U.S. soldiers shot and killed the Sioux leader Sitting Bull while trying to **arrest** him. The rest of the Sioux fled, but the soldiers chased them. At Wounded Knee in South Dakota, soldiers shot and killed more than 200 Sioux.

---

captured: caught and took as a prisoner
starvation: having no food
arrest: take to prison

> ## LANGUAGE TIP
> **Pluperfect**
>
> The pluperfect tense describes something that happened in the past before another action. Use *had* + verb.
>
> **Native Americans *had* lived in North America before the Europeans arrived.**
>
> **Many people *had* died from cold and starvation (before the soldiers came).**

▲ The Battle of Wounded Knee

Before You Go On

1. Where did the U.S. government want to put Native Americans? Why?
2. Where did Chief Joseph and the Nez Percé flee to?
3. In what other ways could the U.S. government have handled the Native Americans?

WORLD EVENTS

1890 First general elections held in Japan

1891 Young Turk movement is formed in Turkey

UNIT EVENTS

1879 Thomas Edison invents lightbulb

1883 Brooklyn Bridge opens; is longest bridge in world

1890 National American Woman Suffrage Association formed

1892 Ellis Island opens in New York Harbor

The Industrial Age

Railroads were important during the Civil War. They took the soldiers to the battlefields. They moved materials to and from the factories. They were important for the growth of industry in the United States. Railroad travel became safer and faster. Railroad companies built thousands of miles of new tracks. This created thousands of new jobs for steelworkers, coal miners, and lumberjacks. The economy grew.

Some people became very rich. Cornelius Vanderbilt made a fortune in shipping and railroads. John D. Rockefeller made a **fortune** in the oil industry. Andrew Carnegie made millions in the steel industry, and J. Pierpont Morgan built a huge banking company.

---

fortune: a lot of money

▲ Workers at a steel factory

ELSEWHERE IN THE WORLD

Marie and Pierre Curie

Marie Curie was a Polish scientist. In 1898 she and her French husband, Pierre, discovered two new elements, radium and polonium. Together, Marie and Pierre won a Nobel Prize in 1903. After the death of her husband, Marie continued their work. She studied the X rays these elements made. She also found that they could be used to treat cancer. Marie and Pierre's work is very important in the history of science and medicine.

1894 Rudyard Kipling writes *Jungle Book*

1896 First modern Olympics held in Athens, Greece

1898 Pierre and Marie Curie discover radium and polonium

1900 Boxer Rebellion begins in China

1893 Alexander Graham Bell makes first long-distance telephone call

1896 William McKinley elected president of United States

1898 Spanish-American War begins

The Industrial Revolution changed people's lives in many ways. Before the Industrial Revolution, many people lived in small towns or on farms. Now they moved to the cities to work in the factories. People, including children, worked for twelve to fourteen hours every day. Conditions were very bad, and many people got sick and died.

Many things were invented during this time. By 1900 new inventions included the telephone, the typewriter, the phonograph, the camera, and the electric light. Cars appeared in the streets of cities. Life was changing. The modern age was beginning.

▼ Early lightbulb, telephone, and sewing machine

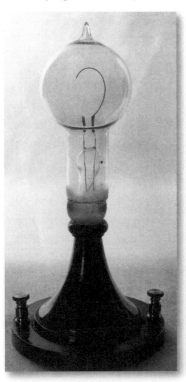

MORE ABOUT IT

The First Cars

Henry Ford's factory in Detroit, Michigan, was the first manufacturer to mass produce cars on a moving assembly line. This system made it possible for workers to build cars in fifteen minutes. Because the factory could make so many cars, the price of a car was low. Ford's most famous car, the Model T, sold for $295 in 1922 (about $3,000 in today's money).

Before You Go On

1. Why were railroads important?
2. Why did people move to the cities?
3. Do you think life was harder in the city than on the farm?

A New Nation **227**

Vocabulary

Choose a word from the box to complete each sentence. Write the sentences in your notebook.

Confederacy	fort	Union
railroads	battle	Mason-Dixon Line

1. The _____ separated Confederate states from Union states.

2. Many soldiers died in an important _____ at Gettysburg.

3. General Robert E. Lee led the army of the _____ .

4. President Lincoln wanted the South to rejoin the _____.

5. Soldiers and other people are protected inside the walls of a _____.

6. _____ moved materials to and from the factories.

Check Your Understanding

Write the answer to each question in your notebook.

1. Which side won the Civil War?

2. What do the Fourteenth and Fifteenth Amendments say?

3. What happened at Little Big Horn?

4. What were some inventions of the Industrial Age?

Apply Social Studies Skills

Content Reading Strategy: Draw Conclusions

Copy the graphic organizer into your notebook. Write the conclusion that you come to after reading the fact in both clues.

Clue 1
After 1869 having cattle walk to markets from Texas to Kansas was no longer necessary.

Clue 2
By 1869 the country's largest railroad was completed.

Conclusion

Using Visuals: **Read a Graph**

Look at the bar graph below to answer the questions in your notebook.

United States Railroads, 1840–1860

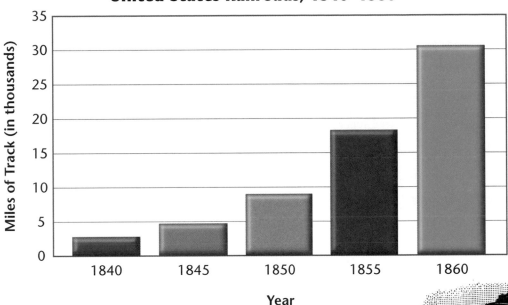

Miles of Track (in thousands)

Year

1. What do the numbers on the left show?
2. How many years does the graph cover?
3. How might the building of railroads affect the economy?
4. What can you conclude from looking at the graph?

Discuss

In a war, a country can make a law that says men must join the army or navy. This law is called a draft. During the Civil War in 1863, Congress passed a draft law in the North. Under the law, a man could avoid the draft by paying the government $300. Do you think this was fair? Give reasons for your opinion.

For more practice,
go to Workbook pages 107–108.

Unit Review

Vocabulary

Choose a word from the box to complete each sentence. Write the sentences in your notebook.

Confederacy	tribe	battle	pioneers
immigrant	industry	Union	Mason-Dixon Line
railroads	fort	wagon train	gold rush

1. In the North many people worked in _____.
2. The _____ fought the Civil War to keep slavery and states' rights.
3. Chief Joseph was the leader of a Native American _____.
4. The _____ won an important battle at Gettysburg.
5. Soldiers were protected inside the walls of a _____.
6. Finding gold in California started the _____.
7. During the Civil War, soldiers traveled to the battlefields on the _____.
8. The Civil War started with a _____ at Fort Sumter.
9. An _____ was a person who moved to America to build the railroads.
10. People who traveled and settled in the West were _____.
11. In 1860 the _____ separated the North and the South.
12. The _____ was a way for pioneers to travel across the Great Plains.

Timeline Check

Put the events in the correct order. Use the timelines in the unit to help you. Write the sentences in your notebook.

_____ The southern states form the Confederacy.

_____ Lewis and Clark explore the land west of the Mississippi River.

_____ President Lincoln is assassinated.

_____ George Washington becomes the first president of the United States.

_____ The Industrial Age begins.

_____ Pioneers travel west on the Oregon Trail.

_____ Congress passes the Fourteenth and Fifteenth Amendments to the Constitution.

Apply Social Studies Skills

Using Visuals: **Read a Graph**

Look at the circle graphs below. The circle graphs for 1800 and 1820 are completed. Make a circle graph in your notebook. Read the information below to complete the circle graph for 1860.

In 1860 there were 243 members in the House of Representatives. Of these, 158 (about two-thirds) came from free states; 85 of these (about one-third) came from slave states.

1800
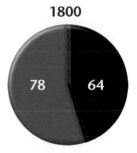
78   64

Total members = 142

1820
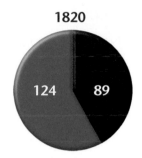
124   89

Total members = 213

1860
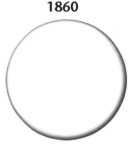

Total members = 243

 Representatives from northern states

 Representatives from southern states

Extension Project

Find out how many United States presidents were in office between George Washington and Abraham Lincoln. Put them in a timeline.

Read More About It

Look for these books in the library.

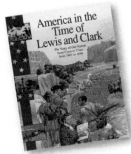

▲ *America in the Time of Lewis and Clark* by Sally Senzell Isaacs

▲ *Civil War* by John Stanchak

◀ *Journey to Ellis Island: How My Father Came to America* by Carol Bierman

For more practice, go to Workbook pages 109–110.

Writing Skills

Revise a Three-Paragraph Essay

A good writer rereads his or her first draft and thinks about how to make it better. The way to make your essay better is to revise it. When you revise your essay, you change it. These are some questions you should ask yourself.

- Is my main idea stated clearly?
- Are my ideas in the best order?
- Did I use specific details and examples?
- Does my draft have a beginning, a middle, and an end?
- Are all my sentences related to the topic?

Read the student's essay below. Notice how parts of the essay are crossed out.

Uses of the Buffalo

Native American tribes of the Great Plains needed the buffalo to live. The Plains Indians used the buffalo for food, clothing, and shelter. They made dried ~~meat~~ strips with the meat from the buffalo. The Plains Indians hunted all year long. The buffalo was cooked over a fire and dried in the sun. ~~and made into jerky.~~ They also made dried meat into powder and mixed it with melted fat.

Women made clothes with the buffalo hide. For example, they made robes, moccasins, snowshoes, and carrying bags. They made sewing thread from the long muscles of the buffalo. Buffalo skins were used to make the Plains Indians' houses, called teepees. ~~Also as blankets. By 1889 there were only 550 buffalo left alive in all the United States.~~

The buffalo was very important to the Plains Indians. The meat of the buffalo was high in protein. No part of a buffalo was thrown away. Without the buffalo the Plains tribes had little food, poor shelter, and no warm clothing. Their way of life would change.

Talk with a classmate about why some parts were crossed out. Did the student answer all the questions listed above?

Practice

Write a three-paragraph essay on a topic from this unit. Then revise it.

or

Revise the three-paragraph essay you wrote at the end of Unit 5.

Remember to ask yourself the questions on page 232 before you revise your work.

▲ Hunting buffalo

For more practice, go to Workbook pages 111–112.

WORLD'S HIGHEST STANDARD OF LIVING

There's no way like the American Way

Unit Contents

People

- Susan B. Anthony and Emmeline Pankhurst
- Archduke Franz Ferdinand
- Woodrow Wilson
- Franklin D. Roosevelt
- Adolf Hitler
- John F. Kennedy

- Martin Luther King Jr.
- Mikhail Gorbachev
- Ronald Reagan
- Richard Nixon
- Bill Clinton
- Nelson Mandela
- Saddam Hussein

Places

- Pearl Harbor, Hawaii
- Nagasaki and Hiroshima
- Soviet Union
- Korea

- Cuba
- Vietnam
- Chile
- South Africa
- Persian Gulf

Key Events

- World Wars I and II
- The Great Depression
- The Cold War
- Wars in Korea and Vietnam
- The Soviet Union breaks up
- Apartheid ends
- The Gulf Wars

Get Ready

In your notebook, draw a timeline like the one here. Write an event from Unit 6 for each date.

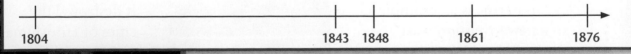

1804   1843 1848   1861   1876

235

Vocabulary

◀ A **dictator** is a leader who has absolute power. Adolf Hitler was a dictator in Germany.

▲ An **assassination** is a murder for political reasons. World War I began when Archduke Franz Ferdinand of Austria-Hungary was assassinated.

▲ During World War II, the Nazis put many Jews and others in concentration camps. They killed many of these people. This large killing is called the **Holocaust**.

▲ **Submarines** are boats that can travel underwater. A submarine is an example of a new invention used during World War I.

◀ The **atomic bomb** was the most deadly weapon used in World War II. It destroyed the cities of Hiroshima and Nagasaki.

▲ During the Great Depression many people did not have work. They waited in long lines hoping to get jobs. **Unemployment** is when many people don't have jobs.

Key Words

assassination

atomic bomb

dictator

Holocaust

submarines

unemployment

Practice

Choose the word that completes each sentence. Write the sentences in your notebook.

1. A boat that can travel underwater is called a ________.
   a. dictator b. submarine c. atomic bomb
2. An ________ is a murder, usually for political reasons.
   a. assassination b. dictator c. unemployment
3. The ________ was a mass killing of people during World War II.
   a. unemployment b. submarine c. Holocaust
4. When a lot of people are without work, there is ________.
   a. submarine b. assassination c. unemployment
5. A leader of a country who controls everything is a ________.
   a. submarine b. dictator c. Holocaust
6. An ________ is a weapon that can kill many people.
   a. atomic bomb b. assassination c. submarine

Workbook

For more practice, go to Workbook page 113.

Social Studies Skills

Content Reading Strategy: **Summarize**

When you **summarize** information, you say it or write it in a shorter form. You use fewer words. To write a summary:

- read the *information* you are going to summarize
- find the *main idea*
- find the *most important details*
- write the main idea and the most important details *in your own words*

For example, read the paragraph about Cuba. Then read the summary below the paragraph. The main idea and the most important details have been summarized.

Paragraph

At the beginning of the Spanish-American War in 1898, the United States told Cuba that it would be an independent country when the war was over. When the Spanish-American War ended, the United States changed its mind. Should Cuba be an independent country or part of the United States? Finally, the United States gave Cuba some independence. Cuba wrote its own constitution. However, the United States kept some control over Cuba. The United States wrote an amendment to Cuba's constitution which said the United States had the right to come into Cuba. The United States also took control of a naval base in Cuba.

Summary

The United States promised Cuba that it would be independent from the United States after the Spanish-American War. But the United States did not keep its promise. Cuba wrote its own constitution, but it had to let the United States come into Cuba and control a naval base.

**For more practice,
go to Workbook pages 114–115.**

Building Research Skills: **Use Print Resources**

The library has many sources of information called reference tools. These tools help you research, or find the information you need or want to know. Here are some reference tools:

- An **encyclopedia** is a set of books with articles about many different subjects. The subjects are arranged in alphabetical order.

- A **dictionary** is a collection of words with their meanings, spellings, and pronunciations. The words are arranged in alphabetical order.

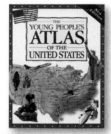

- An **atlas** is a book of maps. There are different kinds of maps, and some atlases specialize in one kind of map.

- **Periodicals** are newspapers and magazines published on a regular basis, such as every week or every month. Most libraries have a periodicals section.

Answer the questions in your notebook about which reference tool you would use.

1. Where would you look to find out what happened in the Middle East last week?

2. Where would you look to find the capital of Russia?

3. Where would you look to find information about the Holocaust?

4. Where would you look to find the meaning and pronunciation of the word *allies*?

For more practice, go to Workbook page 116.

Reading ❶

The Progressive Era

Americans did not want the countries of Europe to become powerful in the New World. In 1898 the United States went to war against Spain. The Spanish-American War lasted only four months. The United States won.

After signing a treaty with Spain, the United States **acquired** Puerto Rico and Guam. The United States also paid Spain $20 million for the Philippines.

As the twentieth century began, Americans felt hopeful. This time period became known as the Progressive Era. Industrial production was increasing. There were many new inventions. But at the same time, there was a need to **reform** working conditions in factories.

---

acquired: got; obtained
reform: change for the better

▲ A young boy working in a canning factory in the early twentieth century

CONNECT TO TODAY

The Food and Drug Administration

Around the beginning of the twentieth century, the meat industry in the United States was bad. Sick animals were killed and sold for food. Some meat even contained rat meat!

In 1906 President Theodore Roosevelt convinced Congress to pass the Pure Food and Drug Act.

Today, the Food and Drug Administration oversees the production of food and medicines. All food products must have their ingredients listed on the package.

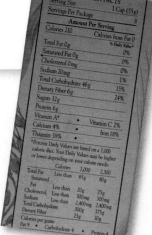

1910 Mexican
Revolution begins

1911 Chinese
Revolution begins

1916 Easter
Uprising in Ireland

1919 Swedish women
granted full suffrage

1906 Congress
passes Pure Food
and Drug Act

1913 Henry Ford
begins assembly-line
manufacturing

1920 Women in U.S.
win right to vote

In the 1800s and early 1900s, women in many Western countries **demanded** the right to vote. The right to vote is called suffrage. There were many women's suffrage movements and great leaders, such as Susan B. Anthony in the United States and Emmeline Pankhurst in Great Britain. They organized protests and **lobbied** politicians. In 1893 New Zealand became the first country in the world to give women suffrage. In 1902 Australian women could vote in national elections. Swedish women with property could vote in city elections in 1862. Sweden **granted** women full suffrage in 1919. In the United States, women won the right to vote in 1920. In Britain, women over thirty won the right to vote in 1918, and full suffrage in 1928.

---

demanded: asked strongly for something
lobbied: tried to influence
granted: gave

As You Read

Summarize

Work with a classmate. Retell what you just read about the Progressive Era in your own words.

▲ Emmeline Pankhurst was arrested in London while protesting for women's suffrage.

Before You Go On

1. Who won the Spanish-American War?

2. Why do you think the factories needed reforms?

3. What was women's suffrage?

World War I

World War I, also known as the Great War, started in 1914 after the assassination of Archduke Franz Ferdinand and his wife Sophie of Austria-Hungary. This assassination was the **spark** that caused all of Europe and, eventually, the United States to go to war.

Germany, the Austro-Hungarian Empire, and Turkey—called the Central Powers—wanted to **expand** their control in Europe. Great Britain, France, Russia, and Belgium—called the **Allies**—were against them. The Central Powers and the Allies began to fight each other for power.

---

spark: the thing that makes something happen
expand: get larger
allies: countries that are united for the same cause

MORE ABOUT IT

Weapons of War

World War I was the first modern war. There were new weapons, such as submarines (underwater ships) and machine guns that shot many bullets very quickly. Gas masks protected soldiers from poisonous gases. Tanks had big guns and armor over their wheels. They were difficult to destroy. New fighter airplanes were small and had machine guns.

▼ Europe, 1918

KEY

- Allied Powers, 1918
- Central Powers, 1918
- Neutral countries
- ⚔ Battle sites
- — National border
- • City

▲ A World War I soldier

1917 Bolshevik Revolution begins in Russia

1918 Women over 30 get vote in Great Britain

1919 New Zealand scientist splits atom

1920 Allies divide Ottoman Empire

1916 Woodrow Wilson elected to second term

1917 U.S. enters World War I

1918 World War I ends; Wilson creates 14 Point Plan for Peace

1919 Wilson helps form League of Nations

1920 Prohibition begins

The United States wanted to be **neutral**. But in 1917 Germany attacked U.S. ships. President Woodrow Wilson and the Congress declared war on Germany. The United States joined the Allies. During the war, more than 8 million soldiers were killed on both sides, and more than 20 million were wounded. But Germany became weak. In November 1918, Germany agreed to stop fighting. The Allies had won.

The Allies met in France and wrote a peace treaty called the Treaty of Versailles. President Wilson helped form the League of Nations. France and Great Britain joined. However, the United States Congress wanted to stay out of Europe's **quarrels**. The United States did not join.

---

neutral: not taking sides
quarrels: arguments; fights

▼ World War I battlefield

CONNECT TO
TODAY

United Nations

After World War I, people wanted to prevent another war. President Wilson helped form the League of Nations in 1919 to help solve world problems that might lead to war. But when World War II started in 1939, the League of Nations ended. After World War II, the United Nations was created. Like the League of Nations, the purpose of the United Nations was to help solve world problems. This time, the United States joined.

Today, 191 countries are represented at the United Nations.

Before You Go On

1. What event sparked World War I?
2. Who were Britain's allies against the Central Powers?
3. Why do you think President Wilson did not want the United States to go to war?

The Modern World **243**

The Great Depression

After World War I, times were good in the United States for a while. The 1920s were called the Roaring Twenties or the Jazz Age. People were glad the war was over and **optimistic** about the future.

Then in 1929 the **stock market** fell apart and many people lost all of their money. This event was the beginning of the Great **Depression**. Banks lost money. Unemployment was high. One in four Americans did not have a job. Franklin D. Roosevelt was elected president of the United States in 1932. He created a set of programs called the New Deal to end the Great Depression.

---

optimistic: hopeful
stock market: a way of trading stocks and shares
depression: a period when the economy is poor

MORE ABOUT IT

The New Deal

President Roosevelt wanted to help people get back to work. His New Deal programs were called the Alphabet Soup Agencies and Acts. Some of these were the FHA (Federal Housing Act), the NYA (National Youth Administration), and the WPA (Works Progress Administration). The programs helped the United States recover. People became optimistic again.

◀ People wait in line for bread and canned food during the Depression.

- **1931** Japan invades China
- **1932** Franklin Roosevelt elected president
- **1933** Roosevelt creates New Deal programs
- **1935** Italy invades Ethiopia
- **1935** Social Security Act becomes law
- **1936** Spanish Civil War begins
- **1939** France and Great Britain declare war on Germany
- **1941** Japan bombs Pearl Harbor; U.S. enters World War II

World War II

After World War I, Germany went into an economic depression. Germany's leader, Adolf Hitler, was a dictator and the head of the **Nazi Party**. Hitler blamed France and Great Britain for the depression. Germans supported the Nazi Party because they thought it offered hope for the future. Germany began to rebuild its army.

In 1939 Germany invaded Poland. Great Britain and France declared war on Germany. World War II began in Europe. In 1940 Italy and Japan joined Germany. The three countries were called the Axis Powers.

On December 7, 1941, Japan bombed Pearl Harbor in Hawaii. The United States declared war on Japan. Germany and Italy then declared war on the United States.

Nazi Party: a political party

▼ **Europe, 1942**

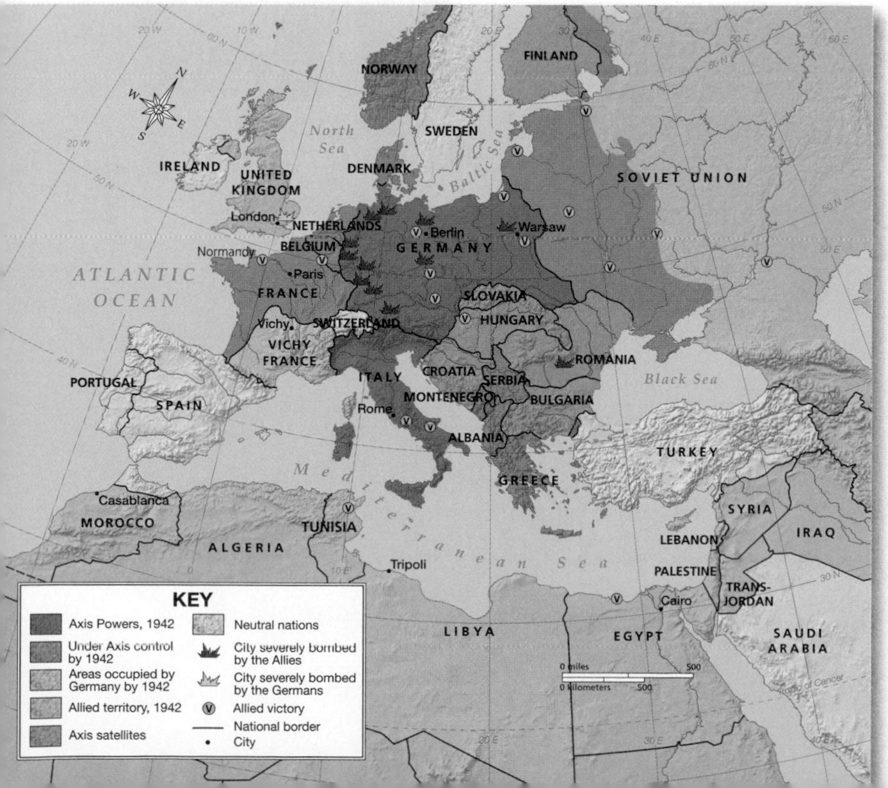

MORE ABOUT IT

Internment Camps

After Japan bombed Pearl Harbor, the U.S. government forced Japanese-Americans to leave their homes. The government thought they might be spies for Japan. About 110,000 Japanese-Americans lived in internment camps. They had to stay there until the war ended.

In 1988 the government apologized to Japanese-Americans and paid money to camp survivors.

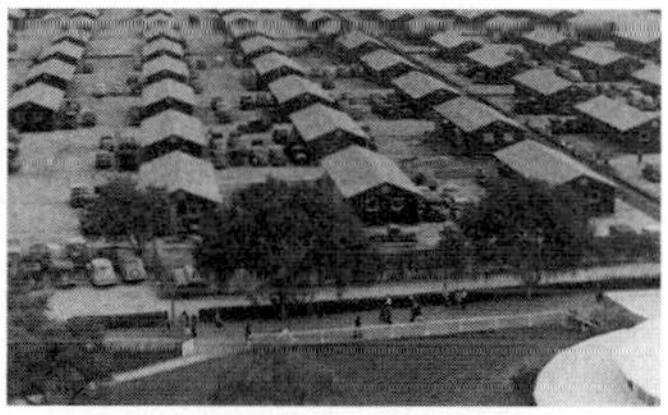

Before You Go On

1. What event started the Great Depression?
2. What event started World War II?
3. Why were the New Deal programs called the Alphabet Soup Agencies and Acts?

Primary Source

Franklin D. Roosevelt's Speech

In January, 1941, World War II had already begun in Europe. France had fallen to the German army. Hitler's airplanes were also bombing Great Britain.

President Franklin Roosevelt knew the United States might have to enter the war. He wanted to prepare the American people. During his 1941 State of the Union address, he tried to explain why it was important to fight for freedom.

Below is a passage from this speech. As you read, look for words you know. They will help you understand the passage.

In . . . future days . . . we look forward to a world founded upon four human freedoms.

The first is freedom of speech—everywhere in the world.

The second is freedom of every person to worship God in his own way—everywhere in the world.

The third is freedom from want—which . . . will secure to every nation a healthy peacetime life for its [people] everywhere in the world.

The fourth is freedom from fear, which . . . means [reducing weapons] to such a point . . . that no nation will be in a position to [attack its] neighbor anywhere in the world.

This nation has placed its [future] in the hands, heads, and hearts of millions of free men and women. . . . Our support goes to those who [fight] to gain those rights and keep them.

1. What was happening in Europe when President Roosevelt made his 1941 State of the Union address?

2. What are the four freedoms that Roosevelt felt were worth fighting for?

1942 Torpedo guidance system invented by actress Hedy Lamarr and composer George Antheil

1943 Race riots in New York City, Los Angeles, and Detroit

1944 Germany develops first missile

1945 Atomic bomb invented

1942 Manhattan Project begins

1943 Warsaw Ghetto uprising

1944 Invasion of Normandy

1945 World War II ends

By 1945 the Allies won back Europe. Germany surrendered. The world learned that Hitler and the Nazis had murdered 12 million people during the Holocaust. After the surrender of Germany, the Allies fought to end the war with Japan in the Pacific.

On August 6 and 9, 1945, U.S. bombers dropped two atomic bombs on Japan, in Hiroshima and Nagasaki. On August 14, Japan finally surrendered. The war was over. That same year, representatives of fifty countries met to sign the United Nations Charter. The purpose was to **prevent** future wars and to have nations help each other.

---

prevent: stop from happening

SCIENCE CONNECTION

The Manhattan Project

In 1942 a top-secret project, called the Manhattan Project, brought together important scientists to develop an atomic bomb. The bomb was based on the scientific principle of nuclear fission. Nuclear fission releases a lot of heat energy. The atomic bomb was much stronger than anyone thought it would be. Some of the scientists were later sorry they created such a terrible weapon.

◀ The Japanese city of Hiroshima was destroyed at the end of World War II.

Before You Go On

1. Who was Adolf Hitler?
2. What event ended World War II?
3. How do you think the world reacted to the atomic bomb explosions?

Vocabulary

Choose a word from the box to complete each sentence. Write the sentences in your notebook.

assassination	submarines	Holocaust
dictator	atomic bomb	unemployment

1. During the Great Depression, _____ was a huge problem.

2. The Germans used _____ in World War I.

3. The United States dropped an _____ on Hiroshima at the end of World War II.

4. The _____ of a leader started World War I.

5. Adolf Hitler was a _____ who started World War II.

6. The killing of millions of people in Germany was called the _____ .

Check Your Understanding

Write the answer to each question in your notebook.

1. What happened during the Progressive Era?

2. What happened in 1929 that changed many people's lives?

3. What event made President Wilson decide to go to war?

4. Who were the Axis Powers and who were the Allies in World War II?

Apply Social Studies Skills

Content Reading Strategy: **Summarize**

Summarize what you know about World War I. Make sure you include the most important points that you learned. Make sure your summary has a beginning, a middle, and an end.

Building Research Skills: **Use Print Resources**

In what print resource would you find each of the following? Write the answers in your notebook.

1. **de•pres•sion** /di-ˈpre-shən/ *noun* 1 a feeling of sadness and a loss of hope 2 a long period when businesses are not very active and many people do not have jobs 3 an area of a surface that is lower than the other parts

2. **Women's Suffrage** is the right of women to vote. Women who wanted equal rights formed national organizations. One group was called the National Woman Suffrage Association. It was led by Elizabeth Cady Stanton and Susan B. Anthony. Some members of this group tried to vote in the 1872 presidential election. Some of the women were arrested. Some went on a hunger strike in jail. Susan B. Anthony made a speech for women's rights at her trial in Rochester, New York.

3.

4. **Miami, Florida** Emergency officials changed their focus today from search and rescue to relief efforts after Hurricane Edward cut a destructive path through the state. Beachfront homes were destroyed, roofs were blown off, and poles snapped in two, leaving power lines in the streets. The storm made landfall late Thursday with 150 m.p.h. winds. Nearly 700 people are reported homeless. About 75 percent of residents are without power, and at least 2,500 people are in shelters, local officials said. Edward is the third hurricane to hit Florida this season.

Discuss

Today we take for granted many of the things that people fought for in history. To take something for granted means to think that it has always been there and will always be there. For example, today some people take for granted the right to vote. However, many people struggled their entire lives so that men and women of all races could vote. Do you think voting is important? Explain.

For more practice, go to Workbook pages 117–118.

Vocabulary

Communism is a political system in which the government controls everything in a country, such as factories, farms, and businesses. People can't own property or practice religion freely. ▼

▲ **Democracy** is a system of government in which each person can vote to elect a leader. People can own property and practice any religion freely. The government does not have complete control over the **economy**. The economy is the money, business, and products in a country.

◄ The **resources** of a country are very important for its economy. Many countries have natural resources. Natural resources such as oil, diamonds, coal, and gold come from the earth. Countries use these resources to trade and become richer.

Key Words

communism

democracy

economy

global

resources

terrorism

▲ **Terrorism** is a violent political action by a person or a group of people. Acts of terrorism include kidnapping, car bombing, suicide bombing, assassination, and hijacking (taking control of airplanes). These actions are done to cause terror or fear in a society, for revenge, or to try to change a political situation. Terrorism occurs in many countries around the world. It is a **global** threat.

Practice

Choose the word that completes each sentence. Write the sentences in your notebook.

1. _____ is a political system in which people can't own property or businesses.

   a. Democracy   **b.** Communism   **c.** Economy

2. Gold, silver, oil, and land are _____.

   a. economy   **b.** terrorism   **c.** resources

3. _____ is a system of government in which people vote to elect their leaders.

   a. Democracy   **b.** Communism   **c.** Economy

4. A violent political action by a person or group is called _____.

   a. communism   **b.** terrorism   **c.** resources

5. _____ means something that involves the whole world.

   a. Economy   **b.** Global   **c.** Democracy

6. Money, resources, and businesses are part of a country's _____.

   a. terrorism   **b.** global   **c.** economy

For more practice, go to Workbook page 119.

Social Studies Skills

Content Reading Strategy: **Understand Fact and Opinion**

A **fact** is a statement that is true and you can check. An **opinion** tells about personal feeling. It cannot be proved true or false.

Facts and opinions help you understand the world you live in. Many writers use fact and opinion when they write. A fact can support the writer's argument. An opinion can make facts more interesting.

To tell the difference between a fact and an opinion:

- read the passage carefully

- ask yourself what statements can be proved. You can use resources like encyclopedias and maps to check facts.

- ask yourself what statements cannot be proved. These are opinions. You can look for words such as *believe, think, feel, might,* and *perhaps.* Some writers use *in my opinion.*

Read this passage and then answer the questions below in your notebook.

Television in the 1950s

Television changed American life. Before television, many people read magazines and books, and listened to the radio. In 1950 only about 9 percent of households had a TV. By 1960 about 87 percent of households had a TV. Many people believed that watching a TV was something that a family should do together. The family watched the same program. Today, most families own more than one TV. Perhaps this is because parents and children like to watch different programs.

1. List two facts about television in the 1950s.
2. List an opinion about television in the 1950s.
3. Where can you check the facts in the passage?
4. How do you know which sentence shows an opinion?

**For more practice,
go to Workbook pages 120–121.**

Building Research Skills: **Use Technology Resources**

Libraries have many different kinds of technology resources.

- A **CD-ROM** stores information such as photographs, videos, text, and sound. Many print resources, such as encyclopedias and almanacs, are also available on CD-ROMs.

- The **Internet** is a computer system that stores information you can find and use. Part of the Internet is the World Wide Web. The best way to use the World Wide Web is with a search engine. A good search engine can help you find information quickly and easily. Remember that not all information on the Internet is correct. The most reliable sites often end with .edu (educational institution), .org (organization), or .gov (government).

- Most libraries now have **computerized catalogs**. This makes it easy to search for a reference book by title, author, or subject. The catalog will tell you if the book is available and where to find it.

For more practice, go to Workbook page 122.

WORLD EVENTS	**1948** Israel becomes nation	**1950** First successful kidney transplant performed	**1954** Algerian war of independence against France begins

UNIT EVENTS	**1950** Korean War begins	**1951** Julius and Ethel Rosenberg executed for spying	**1955** Montgomery, Alabama, bus boycott begins

Reading ②

Democracy vs. Communism

During World War II, the Soviet Union, the United States, and Great Britain worked together. However, soon after the war, a conflict of **ideology** developed. The Soviet Union had a communist government. The United States and Great Britain had democratic governments. The Soviet Union built up a strong army and did not allow its people to visit countries with democratic governments. An **invisible** line called the Iron Curtain divided the Soviet Union from the West.

---

ideology: political beliefs and ideas
invisible: not able to be seen

MORE ABOUT IT

The Berlin Wall

In 1961 the Soviets built a wall across the city of Berlin and a barrier across Germany, dividing East from West. Soldiers guarded the Berlin Wall. Anyone who tried to cross the wall might be shot. The wall divided families and friends for 28 years. During that time 5,000 people successfully escaped from East Berlin to the West. The most common escape was by digging a tunnel under the wall.

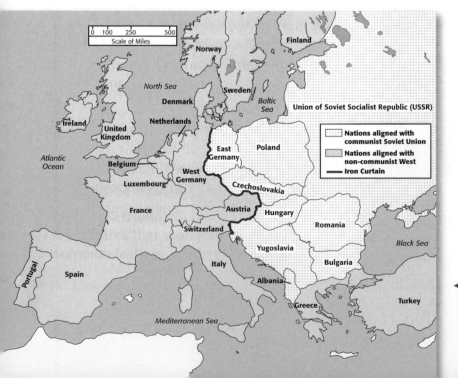

◀ Europe after World War II

1959
Cuban Revolution
takes place

1964 China explodes
its first atomic bomb

1966 Cultural Revolution
takes place in China

1968 Soviet
Union invades
Czechoslovakia

1957 School integration
in Little Rock, Arkansas

1961 Soviets
build Berlin Wall

1963 President John F.
Kennedy assassinated

1968 Tet Offensive
takes place in Vietnam

The Cold War

The period of time when communist governments and democratic governments did not **trust** each other was called the Cold War. It began after World War II and ended in the early 1990s. During the Cold War, the United States and its allies tried to spread democracy around the world. The Soviet Union and its allies tried to spread communism to countries such as Korea and Vietnam. The United States and the Soviet Union did not fight in a war, but they came very close to it. The Soviet Union's desire to spread communism to other countries led to the United States' **involvement** in wars in Korea and Vietnam.

---

trust: believe that someone is honest
involvement: taking part

◀ Children take cover under their desks during an air raid drill in Ohio.

MORE ABOUT IT

The Cuban Missile Crisis

After Cuba became communist under Fidel Castro, the Soviets put missiles in Cuba. President John F. Kennedy responded by sending U.S. Navy ships to the waters near Cuba. It was a tense 13 days before Soviet leader Khrushchev agreed to remove the missiles. The conflict ended peacefully, but many people were worried about the possibility of nuclear war.

Before You Go On

1. How are democracy and communism different?
2. Why did the United States get involved in wars in Korea and Vietnam?
3. Why do you think the invisible line between Europe and the Soviet Union was called the "Iron Curtain"?

The Modern World **255**

WORLD EVENTS

1964 Nelson Mandela sentenced to life in prison in South Africa

1969 U.S. astronaut Neil Armstrong walks on the moon

1971 Idi Amin takes power in Uganda

UNIT EVENTS

1964 Martin Luther King Jr. gets Nobel Peace Prize

1968 Martin Luther King Jr. assassinated; Robert F. Kennedy assassinated

1969 My Lai massacre in Vietnam

1973 U.S. leaves Vietnam

The Vietnam Era

In the 1960s, Vietnam, a country in Southeast Asia, was divided into two countries, North Vietnam and South Vietnam. The North was communist and the South was not. North Vietnamese communists, along with South Vietnamese rebels, called the Viet Cong, wanted to unite the country under one communist government. The United States and its allies sent money and troops to help South Vietnam. The United States fought the Viet Cong.

Many people in the United States and around the world thought the war was wrong. There were protests and demonstrations against the U.S. government. In 1973, after many years of fighting and many deaths, the United States finally left Vietnam. Vietnam became one communist country.

SCIENCE CONNECTION

The Space Race

The United States and the Soviet Union were in close competition to send a man into space. On April 12, 1961, Yuri Gagarin, a Soviet astronaut, was successfully launched into space. The next month the United States sent Alan Shepard into space in the *Freedom 7* spacecraft.

Profile

Martin Luther King Jr.

Martin Luther King Jr. was born in 1929 in Atlanta, Georgia. He experienced racism early in life. He decided to do something to make the world a better and fairer place. After graduating from college and getting married, he became a minister and moved to Alabama.

During the 1950s, Martin Luther King began to work for civil rights. Dr. King and other African-American leaders led a successful boycott of the Montgomery, Alabama, segregated bus system. In the early 1960s, Dr. King took part in many other peaceful protests against the unfair treatment of African Americans. He won the Nobel Peace Prize in 1964. Dr. King was assassinated on April 4, 1968, in Memphis, Tennessee. Today, to honor the life of this important leader, we celebrate Martin Luther King Day each year in January.

1979
Mother Teresa gets
Nobel Peace Prize

1981 AIDS virus
first identified

1984 Indian Prime Minister
Indira Gandhi assassinated

1989 Communist
government overthrown
in Romania

1990
Nelson Mandela
freed from prison

1980 Ronald Reagan
elected president

1985 Mikhail Gorbachev
becomes new leader of
Soviet Union

1991 Communism
ends in Soviet Union;
Berlin Wall torn down

The Soviet Union Breaks Up

LANGUAGE TIP

Phrasal Verbs

A verb + a particle =
a phrasal verb.

The meanings of the
separate words are
different from the meaning
of the phrasal verb.

break up
break down
break in
break through

In 1985 the Soviet Union had a new leader called Mikhail Gorbachev. President Gorbachev wanted to improve his country's economy, which was **failing** when he came to power. He thought it was time for great social changes. He wanted to end the Cold War and to trade with Western countries. President Gorbachev met with U.S. President Ronald Reagan.

Finally, in 1991, communism ended in the Soviet Union. The Cold War was over. The Berlin Wall was **torn down**. The Soviet Union divided into many countries. Russia is the largest country that was formerly part of the Soviet Union.

---

failing: not succeeding
torn down: destroyed

▲ President Reagan and President Gorbachev at the White House in Washington, D.C.

Before You Go On

1. Why was there a war in Vietnam?

2. Why did Gorbachev want to change the Soviet Union?

3. Martin Luther King Jr. fought for civil rights. Are there any rights people fight for today?

Central and South America

Many countries in Central and South America have experienced political changes in the past thirty years. Armed conflicts and civil wars removed dictators in countries such as El Salvador, Nicaragua, Guatemala, and Brazil.

In 1973 in Chile, the democratically elected **socialist** president Salvador Allende was overthrown in a **coup** organized by military leader Augusto Pinochet. President Allende was murdered. Nearly 100,000 people were **rounded up** after the coup. During the following ten years at least 3,000 people were murdered and over 100,000 were tortured. Finally, in 1990 the military leader President Pinochet agreed to an election. He lost.

The economies of most Latin American countries are growing, but they are heavily **in debt** to the World Bank.

---

socialist: belonging to a political system similar to communism
coup: an act whereby citizens or the army take over the government
rounded up: brought together by force
in debt: owing money

ELSEWHERE IN THE WORLD

European Union
After World War II, several nations in Europe decided to form the Common Market. Its purpose was to help the European community increase trade and allow workers and money to move freely. In the 1990s these nations changed the name to the European Union (EU) and added more members. In 2004 there were 25 member nations. The EU now has one official currency called the euro.

◄ A soldier watches political prisoners held at the National Stadium in Santiago, Chile, in 1973.

1982 British fight Argentina in Falklands War

1986 Nuclear disaster in Chernobyl, Ukraine

1988 U.S. Air Force unveils stealth bomber

1990 Common Market changes name to European Union

1981 First personal computer introduced

1989 Massacre in Tiananmen Square, Beijing, China

Asia

Japan has a strong economy. It is a rich country. During World War II, the United States dropped two atomic bombs on Japan. After the war, the United States helped Japan rebuild. By the 1970s, Japan became a leader in manufacturing automobiles, computers, and electronics.

China is a communist country. It has a strong economy. President Richard Nixon visited China in 1972 to **improve** the relationship between China and the United States. He succeeded. But in 1989 relations worsened after a **massacre** in Tiananmen Square in Beijing, the capital. Many Chinese protesters who wanted democracy were killed. Then in 1998 President Bill Clinton went to China to improve the relationship again.

improve: make better
massacre: the killing of many people at one time

CONNECT TO
TODAY

China's Challenges

Since 1978 the People's Republic of China has been changing from a centrally planned economy, where the government controls everything, to an economy where there are private businesses. The government has focused on foreign trade as an important way to increase economic growth. With 1.3 billion people, China is the world's most populous country. It is still a communist country.

◀ A Chinese protestor blocks a line of tanks in Tiananmen Square.

Before You Go On

1. What happened in Chile in 1973?
2. Which countries in Asia have strong economies?
3. If you were president of a country in Latin America or Asia, how would you help the economy to grow?

| WORLD EVENTS | **1950** China and Soviet Union sign mutual defense treaty | **1953** Edmund Hillary and Tenzing Norgay reach top of Mt. Everest | **1957** Soviets launch *Sputnik I*, first earth-orbiting satellite; the Space Age begins | **1963** President Kennedy assassinated in Dallas, Texas | **1967** Arab-Israeli Six-Day War |

| UNIT EVENTS | **1956** Morocco becomes independent from France | **1960** Zaire and Congo become independent from Belgium | **1963** Kenya becomes independent from Great Britain |

Africa

The governments of most countries in Africa declared themselves independent from their colonial rulers after World War II. Military dictators, who were not elected by the people, ruled most of these countries. By the early 1990s, however, many countries in Africa allowed the people to elect their leaders.

Africa is made up of hundreds of **ethnic groups**. This has sometimes caused conflict, civil war, and even **genocide** in countries such as Rwanda, Angola, Sierra Leone, and Sudan.

Africa has natural resources such as oil and diamonds, but most countries in Africa are still very poor. Governments and people in Africa want to continue to improve their economy and way of life.

---

ethnic groups: groups that share the same culture or race though not necessarily the same country
genocide: murder of a race of people or of an ethnic group

MORE ABOUT IT

Apartheid

From 1948 until 1994, South Africa had a policy of apartheid. People were separated and given different rights based on their race. The small population of white people in the country ruled over the majority, black people. Nelson Mandela led the movement to end apartheid. He spent 27 years in prison because of his beliefs. When apartheid finally ended, he became the first democratically elected president of South Africa.

◄ Water is a precious resource in many parts of Africa. Women and girls often have to walk for hours to get water for drinking, cooking, and washing.

1982 First successful artificial heart implanted

1990 Hubble Telescope launched

1994 Almost one million people killed in Rwanda genocide

1997 Hong Kong becomes part of China

2001 Taliban regime collapses in Afghanistan after U.S. bombings

2004 Nearly 300,000 people killed in Indian Ocean tsunami

1980 Iran-Iraq War begins

1990 Iraq invades Kuwait

1994 Apartheid ends in South Africa; Nelson Mandela elected president

2001 Terrorist attacks on World Trade Center and Pentagon

2003 U.S. invades Iraq; President Saddam Hussein removed

The Gulf Wars and Terrorism

Most economies in the world depend upon oil for heat, fuel, and industry. The Middle East or Persian Gulf region has the most oil in the world. There have been three major conflicts in that region involving the country of Iraq. Iraq wanted to **dominate** the region. First it invaded Iran in 1980. Then in 1990 Iraq invaded Kuwait. Both times, Iraq was pushed back and gained nothing. In 2003 a **coalition** of countries, including the United States, Great Britain, and Australia, invaded Iraq to overthrow the president, Saddam Hussein. The Iraqi people elected a democratic government in 2005.

Today the conflicts in the Middle East often involve terrorism. It is a major global threat in the modern world.

---

dominate: control
coalition: a group that unites for a special purpose

As You Read

Understand Fact and Opinion

These statements are all facts. Where can you check to find more facts about the Gulf Wars and terrorism?

▲ U.S. marines topple the statue of Saddam Hussein in Baghdad after he is forced out of government.

Before You Go On

1. What form of government did most African countries have after World War II?

2. What is one reason for conflict in some African countries?

3. Why is oil such an important resource?

The Modern World **261**

Vocabulary

Choose a word from the box to complete each sentence. Write the sentences in your notebook.

terrorism	communism	democracy
resources	global	economy

1. The world is moving toward a _____ economy.

2. The system of government in the United States is a _____.

3. Suicide bombings, assassinations, and hijackings are all acts of _____.

4. _____ is the form of government in Vietnam.

5. Oil and gold are important natural _____.

6. Today, Japan has an industrial _____ that produces electronics and cars.

Check Your Understanding

Write the answer to each question in your notebook.

1. How did the Cold War start? Why did it end?

2. What happened to the former Soviet Union?

3. What kind of economies do China and Japan have today?

4. Why did Iraq invade Iran and Kuwait?

Apply Social Studies Skills

Content Reading Strategy: **Understand Fact and Opinion**

After the attacks in New York and Washington, D.C., on September 11, 2001, President George W. Bush declared the War on Terror. Write a paragraph about what you know about the fight against terrorism. Be sure to include facts and opinions. Make sure your paragraph has a beginning, a middle, and an end.

Building Research Skills: **Use Technology Resources**

You have learned about three technology resources:

- the Internet
- CD-ROMs
- computerized catalogs

Which technology resource would you go to first to find the following, and why?

- a book in a library
- a movie about the life of Martin Luther King Jr.
- the latest information about your community's government
- a movie clip of the fall of the Berlin Wall
- a magazine with an article about the U.S. economy
- the latest pictures taken in space
- sounds and pictures from the 1970s

Discuss

The United Nations is a place where nations can discuss the problems of the world, including war, poverty, and disease. Imagine that you went to the United Nations to talk about a problem. In your opinion, what problem is the most important in the world today? Try to support your opinion with facts.

For more practice, go to Workbook pages 123–124.

Unit Review

Vocabulary

Choose a word from the box to complete each sentence. Write the sentences in your notebook.

atomic bomb	unemployment	global	communism
democracy	dictator	assassination	Holocaust
economy	resources	terrorism	submarines

1. World War I began after the _____ of Archduke Ferdinand.

2. Chile had a military _____ named Pinochet from 1973 to 1990.

3. The Middle Eastern _____ is based on selling oil to other countries.

4. _____ were used for the first time in World War I.

5. A _____ economy means that the world's economies are interconnected.

6. At the end of World War II, the United States dropped an _____ on Hiroshima, Japan.

7. Under _____, the government has complete control over its country's economy.

8. Africa has many natural _____, including diamonds, oil, and gold.

9. Hitler killed millions of people during the _____.

10. In a _____, the people elect their own leaders.

11. _____ is when individuals and groups commit violent political acts.

12. During the Depression, there was a lot of _____ because jobs were difficult to find.

Timeline Check

Put the events in the correct chronological order. Use the timelines in the unit to help you. Write the sentences in your notebook.

_____ Martin Luther King Jr. wins the Nobel Peace Prize

_____ The war in Vietnam ends

_____ Women in the United States win the right to vote

_____ Hiroshima, Japan, is bombed

_____ The Soviet Union breaks up

_____ Iraq invades Iran

_____ World War I begins

Apply Social Studies Skills

Building Research Skills: Use Technology Resources

A search engine is one of the quickest ways to find information on the Internet. A search engine helps you find information by letting you type in a key word or words about the topic. The key words can help you find the exact information you are looking for.

In your notebook, write the key words you would use to start a search of:

- Archduke Ferdinand
- the Great Depression
- the Holocaust
- Pearl Harbor
- John F. Kennedy

Check your key words with a classmate. Use your key words to find information on the Internet using a search engine.

Extension Project

Find out which countries were affected by the tsunami in Southeast Asia on December 26, 2004. Find out what aid they received and how the lives of the people in these countries changed.

Read More About It

Look for these books in the library.

▲ *World War I* by Simon Adams

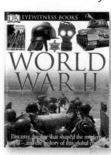

▲ *World War II* by Simon Adams

▲ *Apollo 13* by Dina Anastasio and Brent Furnas

◄ *Nelson Mandela* by Coleen Degnan-Veness

For more practice, go to Workbook pages 125–126.

Writing Skills

Edit and Publish a Three-Paragraph Essay

After you make revisions to your first draft, check your essay for grammar, usage, punctuation, and spelling errors. This is called **editing**. It is sometimes difficult to see all of your mistakes. It can be helpful to have someone else look at your essay and point out errors.

Read the essay below. The marks show the errors. Look at the proofreading marks on the next page to understand what kind of error is marked.

The Spanish Civil War

In 1939 Spain was a divided country. Spain had a dictator called General franco. Franco was a leader strong, His goverment was fascist. This meant that people's lives were completely ruled by the government. Many Spaniards hated Franco. These people formed the Resistance. The Resistance wanted to overthrow Franco's government. Franco was very angry with the resistance.

Germany's dictator, Hitler, supported Franco. Hitler's Nazi Party was also fashist. Franco decided to punish the Resistance. He asked Hitler to help him. On April 26, 1937 Franco ordered nazi planes to bomb the northern Spanish town of Guernica. The bomb killed more than 1,600 peoples and injured nearly 1,000. The artist Pablo Picasso was very shocked and upset by the bombing. He painted a picture called "Guernica." You can see this picture in Spain today. It shows the victims of the war. It is a powerful antiwar statement.

Franco defeated the Resistance. He ruled Spain for many years. Many people were afraid of him. He dies in 1975. Now Spain has a government democratic But Spain will never forgot the terrible civil war that killed one million people and divided the country for a long times.

Proofreading Marks

To:	Use This Mark	Example:
insert something in the text	$\wedge$	We ate rice, bean$_\wedge^s$ and corn.
delete something from the text	ℯ	We ate rice, beans, and corns℘.
close space	⌣	We ⌣ ate rice, beans, and corn.
start a new paragraph	⁋	⁋ We ate rice, beans, and corn.
add a comma	$\wedge$	We ate rice, beans$_\wedge$ and corn.
add a period	⊙	We ate rice, beans, and corn⊙
transpose (switch) letters or words	∿	We ate rice, b$\widetilde{ea}$hs, and corn.
change to a capital letter	$\underline{\underline{a}}$	we ate rice, beans, and corn.
change to a lower case letter	�	WE ate rice, beans, and corn.
let the marked text stand	(stet)	We ate rice, beans, and corn. (stet)

Practice

Now use the essay you wrote in Unit 6 or choose a topic from this unit to write a three-paragraph essay. After completing the essay and making revisions, work with a classmate to edit it. Exchange essays and use the proofreading marks to note the errors. Then make the corrections to your own essay.

Take turns reading your essay aloud with a small group. Read slowly and clearly so that your audience can enjoy your presentation.

For more practice, go to Workbook pages 127–128.

Glossary

Phonetic Respelling Key

a	cat	o	stop
ah	father	oh	go, slow, toe
air	hair, there, their	oo	moon, blue, do
ar	arm	yoo	you, music, few
ay	play, make, eight, they	or	for, your
aw	draw, all, walk	oi	soil, boy
e	red, said	ow	brown, out
ee	green, please, she	u	put, look
eer	ear, here	uh	but, what, from, about, seven
eye	like, right, fly	er	her, work, bird, fur
i	six		

acupuncture (A-kyoo-PUNG-cher)
Traditional Chinese medicine that uses thin needles to treat pain or illness.

agora (A-guh-ruh)
A marketplace in ancient Greece.

agriculture (A-gri-kul-cher)
The growing of crops and raising of animals for people to eat.

American (uh-MER-i-kuhn)
Someone or something from America.

amphitheater (AM-fuh-thee-uh-ter)
A large outdoor theater where plays are performed.

ancient (AYN-shuhnt)
Very old.

apartheid (a-PAR-tayt)
A system in which the different races in a country are separated from each other.

aqueduct (A-kwuh-duhkt)
A structure that brings water into a city.

archaeologist (ar-kee-AH-luh-juhst)
A scientist who studies ancient things and places.

architect (AR-ki-tekt)
Someone whose job is to draw and plan buildings.

assassination (uh-sa-si-NAY-shuhn)
A murder committed for political reasons.

astrolabe (A-stroh-layb)
An early navigation tool that uses the position of the sun, moon, and stars.

atlas (AT-luhs)
A book of maps.

atomic bomb (uh-TAHM-ik bahm)
A very powerful bomb.

atrium (AY-tree-uhm)
A common area in a Roman house that is open to the sky.

battle (BA-tuhl)
A fight between two groups of soldiers.

bay (bay)
A part of the ocean that is enclosed by a curve in the land.

beautiful (BYOO-ti-fuhl)
Very attractive and nice to look at.

Bible (BEYE-buhl)
The Christian holy book.

Bolshevik (BOL-shuh-vik)
A Russian communist.

botany (BAH-tuh-nee)
The scientific study of plants.

British (BRI-tish)
Someone or something from Britain (England, Scotland, Wales, Ireland).

Bubonic plague (byoo-BON-ik playg)
A deadly disease that swept across Europe in the 1340s.

Buddhism (BOO-di-zuhm)
The beliefs and religion based on the teachings of Siddhartha Gautama, or the Buddha.

Byzantine (BIZ-uhn-teen)
Relating to the ancient city of Byzantium (later Constantinople, now Istanbul, Turkey).

canal (kuh-NAL)
A waterway used for irrigation and for boats and ships to pass through.

canyon (KAN-yuhn)
A deep valley with steep sides.

cathedral (kuh-THEE-druhl)
A very large church.

cause and effect (kawz and e-FEKT)
A reading strategy where you look at the cause and effect of something. Why something happens is a cause. What happens is an effect.

chart (chart)
Information that is shown in the form of a graphic. A chart can use pictures and words to help you compare two or more things.

chivalry (SHI-vuhl-ree)
A code of behavior followed by knights in the Middle Ages.

Christianity (kris-tee-AN-uh-tee)
A religion based on the teachings of Jesus Christ.

Christians (KRIS-chuhnz)
People who follow the religion of Christianity.

chronological order
(krah-nuh-LAH ji-kuhl OR-der)
A reading strategy where you think about events in the order in which they happened. A timeline shows dates and events in chronological order.

civilization (siv-uh-luh-ZAY-shuhn)
A way of life in which people have laws, government, and education.

classes (KLA-suhz)
Levels of people in a society, from richest to poorest.

clergy (KLER-jee)
The official leaders within a religious group.

269

climate (KLEYE-muht)
A pattern of weather in a place over a long time.

coast (kohst)
The land next to a sea or an ocean.

cocoa (KOH-koh)
Cocoa beans are the seeds inside the fruit of the cacao tree. The beans are ground to produce chocolate.

colony (KAH-luh-nee)
A country or area that is ruled by another country.

Colosseum (kah-luh-SEE-uhm)
A big outdoor theater in Rome.

communism (KAHM-yoo-ni-zuhm)
A political system in which the government controls everything in a country.

comparatives (kuhm-PAIR-uh-tivz)
Words used to compare two things. To form a comparative, take an adjective and add -er. Example: Argentina is bigger than Peru.

compare and contrast
(kuhm-PAIR and kuhn-TRAST)
A reading strategy where you think about how two things are the same (compare) and how they are different (contrast).

compass rose (KAHM-puhs rohz)
A symbol used to show direction on a map. It is marked north, south, east, and west.

Confederacy (kuhn-FED-er-uh-see)
The name for the southern states during the American Civil War.

Confucianism (kuhn-FYOO-shuhn-iz-uhm)
A religion created by the Chinese teacher Confucius.

conquer (KAHN-ker)
To take over an area or country.

constitution (kahn-sti-TOO-shuhn)
A set of laws governing a country, state, club, etc.

continent (KAHN-ti-nuhnt)
One of the large areas on the earth (Africa, Antarctica, Asia, Australia, Europe, North America, South America).

coup (koo)
An act in which citizens or the army suddenly take control of the government by force.

crops (krahps)
Plants that are grown especially for people and animals to eat.

Crusades (kroo-SAYDS)
A series of military expeditions made by the Christians to try to take Jerusalem back from the Muslims in the Middle Ages.

cuneiform (kyoo-NEE-i-form)
An early form of writing developed by the Sumerians.

daimyo (daym-yoh)
The powerful leader of a clan, or group, of Samurai warriors.

debt (det)
Money, goods, or services owed by one person or government to another.

delta (DEL-tuh)
A low area of land where a river separates into many smaller rivers flowing toward an ocean.

democracy (de-MAH-kruh-see)
A system of government in which each person can vote to elect a leader.

desert (DE-zert)
A large empty area of land where it is hot and dry.

dictator (DIK-tay-ter)
A leader of a country or nation who controls everything. People usually do not like dictators and they are afraid of them. Adolf Hitler was a dictator in Germany.

disease (di-ZEEZ)
An illness or unhealthy condition.

document (DAH-kyoo-muhnt)
A piece of paper that has official information written on it.

drama (DRAH-muh)
Plays acted out for people to watch.

draw conclusions
(draw kuhn-KLOO-zhuhnz)
A reading strategy where you decide what something is about using all the information you have.

drought (drowt)
A long period of time when no rain falls.

dynasty (DEYE-nuh-stee)
A form of government where power is passed down from one family member to another.

east (eest)
One of the four points on a compass rose.

eastern (EEST-ern)
In or from the east part of something or somewhere.

economics (ek-oh-NOM-iks)
The study of the ways that money, goods, and services are made and used.

economy (ee-KAH-nuh-mee)
The money, business, and products of a country.

Enlightenment (en-LEYE-tuhn-muhnt)
A period that began in the 1600s when scientists began to understand more about the world and how things worked.

environmentalist
(en-veye-ruh-MEN-tuh-list)
Someone who is concerned about protecting the environment.

equality (ee-KWAH-li-tee)
The state of having the same conditions, opportunities, and rights as everyone else.

explorer (eks-PLOR-er)
Someone who travels to different places to find out about them.

fact and opinion (fakt and uh-PIN-yuhn)
A reading strategy where you identify fact and opinion. A fact is a statement that is true and can be checked. An opinion tells about personal feeling.

farmer (FAR-mer)
A person who owns or works on a farm where animals or crops are grown for food.

fertile (FER-tuhl)
Good for growing things (for example, crops). Land can be fertile.

festival (FES-tuh-vuhl)
A public celebration.

feudalism (FYOO-duh-li-zuhm)
A social system that formed in Europe during the Middle Ages. Feudalism uses a class system. Kings and lords owned land and ruled over vassals. Vassals ruled over serfs and peasants.

foreigner (FOR-en-er)
A person who comes from another country.

fort (fort)
A group of buildings surrounded by walls and fences to defend people from danger.

French (french)
Someone or something from France.

genocide (JE-noh-seycd)
The planned mass murder of one group by another group for racial, national, or religious reasons.

geography (jee-YAH-gruh-fee)
The study of countries, oceans, mountains, and weather.

glaciers (GLAY-sherz)
Very large areas of ice that move slowly over the ground.

global (GLOH-buhl)
Having to do with the whole world.

globe (glohb)
A ball with a map of the world on it.

gold rush (gohld ruhsh)
An event that occurs after gold is discovered in a place. Many people travel to the place to try to find gold and get rich.

government (GUH-vern-muhnt)
The people who control what happens in a country.

graph (graf)
A way to organize information using numbers and/or pictures.

gulf (gulf)
An area of ocean with land on three sides of it.

hearth (harth)
A fireplace.

heir (air)
Someone who receives a dead person's money, property, or title.

hemisphere (HEM-uhs-feer)
Half of the earth.

hieroglyphics (heye-roh-GLI-fiks)
Written language of pictures developed by the ancient Egyptians.

hill (hil)
An area of high land; a small mountain.

history (HIS-tuh-ree)
The study of things that happened in the past.

holocaust (HOH-luh-kawst)
The killing of millions of Jews and other people by the Nazis during World War II.

holy (HOH-lee)
Relating to God or religion; sacred.

hunter-gatherers (HUHN-ter - GA-ther-erz)
Early humans who hunted animals for food and clothing and gathered plants, seeds, and fruit for food.

immigrant (IM-mi-gruhnt)
A person who moves to a new country to live and work.

indentured servant (in-DEN-cherd SER-vuhnt)
A person who has to work for a certain amount of time to gain freedom.

independence (in-duh-PEN-duhnts)
Political freedom from control by another country.

indigenous (in-DI-juh-nuhs)
A person or thing that has always lived in a place. Native Americans are the indigenous people of the Americas.

industry (IN-duhs-tree)
The business of making things.

Inquisition (in-kwuh-SI-shuhn)
An organization created by the Roman Catholic Church that held trials for people accused of non-Catholic beliefs.

interaction (in-ter-AK-shuhn)
How humans affect the world around them and how the world affects them.

invaders (in-VAY-derz)
People who go into someone else's country and try to take over by force.

irregular verb (eer-REG-yoo-luhr verb)
A verb that does not form the past tense in the usual way. You cannot add *-ed* to an irregular verb. Sometimes letters within the word change. Sometimes the whole word changes.
Example: I am ⟶ I was; I see ⟶ I saw.

irrigation (eer-ri-GAY-shuhn)
A process used in agriculture. Water is taken from places like rivers and used to water crops.

Islam (IZ-lahm)
A religion based on the teachings of Muhammad.

island (EYE-luhnd)
A piece of land surrounded by water.

jujitsu (joo-JIT-soo)
A Japanese method of self defense that does not involve weapons.

justice (JUH-stis)
Treatment of people that is fair and right.

knight (neyet)
A soldier from the Middle Ages.

lake (layk)
A large area of water with land all around it.

latitude (LA-ti-tood)
Imaginary lines that are drawn left and right on maps of the earth.

liberty (LI-ber-tee)
The freedom to do what you want without having to ask permission.

location (loh-KAY-shuhn)
Location answers the question, "Where is it?" It tells you where a place is.

longitude (LAHN-ji-tood)
Imaginary lines that are drawn up and down on maps of the earth.

Lutheranism (LOO-ther-i-ni-zuhm)
A religious movement started by the Roman Catholic monk Martin Luther in the early 1500s.

maize (mayz)
Corn.

manor (MAN-er)
A large village with a large area of land around it.

manuscript (MAN-yoo-skript)
A book written by hand. Before the printing press, books were manuscripts.

map (map)
A drawing of a city, a country, or the world.

map key (map kee)
A list that tells what different symbols or colors mean on a map.

Mason-Dixon Line (MAY-sin DIK-sin leyen)
The line between the northern and southern states during the American Civil War.

massacre (MA-suh-ker)
The act of killing a lot of people at one time.

Mayflower (MAY-flow-er)
The name of the ship on which the Pilgrims sailed to the New World in 1620.

Middle Ages (MID-uhl AY-juhz)
The period in world history between the 400s and the late 1300s.

missionary (MI-shuhn-air-ee)
Someone who goes to a country to teach people about Christianity.

modern (MOD-ern)
Belonging to the present time. Modern history is the period beginning in the early twentieth century.

monitor comprehension
(MAH-ni-ter kahm-pree-HEN-shuhn)
A reading strategy where you check your understanding as you read by looking for clues on the page to help you. Definitions and pictures are helpful.

monument (MAHN-yoo-muhnt)
Something that is built to help people remember an important person or event.

mosque (mahsk)
A building where Muslims go to have religious services.

mound (mownd)
A small hill.

mountain (MOWN-tuhn)
A very high hill.

movable type (MOO-vah-buhl teyep)
Letters of the alphabet used in the printing press to make the production of writing much faster.

movement (MOOV-muhnt)
The study of how people, things, and ideas move from one place to another place.

Muslims (MUZ-luhmz)
People who follow the religion of Islam.

navigation (na-vi-GAY-shuhn)
The science of planning the way from one place to another.

nobles (NOH-buhlz)
People from the upper class; powerful rulers and landowners.

north (north)
One of the four points on a compass rose.

northern (NOR-thern)
In or from the north part of something.

ocean (OH-shuhn)
A very large area of salt water (Arctic Ocean, Atlantic Ocean, Indian Ocean, Pacific Ocean, Antarctic Ocean).

past progressive tense
(past pruh-GRE-siv tens)
A tense used to describe a continuous action that happened in the past. Use the past of *to be* + another verb + - *ing*.

past tense (past tens)
A verb spoken or written in the past.

peasants (PE-zuhnts)
People who had little money and served somebody else.

Peloponnesian War
(pe-loh-poh-NEE-shuhn wor)
The twenty-seven-year war between the ancient Greek city-states of Sparta and Athens.

peninsula (pen-NIN-soo-lah)
A piece of land with water on three sides.

pharaoh (FAIR-roh)
An ancient Egyptian ruler.

philosophy (fi-LAH-suh-fee)
Beliefs and values.

phrasal verb (FRAY-zuhl verb)
A verb whose meaning changes when followed by different prepositions or adverbs.

physical map (FI-zi-kuhl map)
A map that shows what a region looks like, including physical features such as mountains, rivers, and deserts.

pilgrims (PIL-gruhmz)
People who travel to a place for religious reasons.

pioneers (peye-uh-NEERZ)
People who go somewhere or do something before other people.

place (plays)
A description of the physical and human characteristics of an area.

plain (playn)
A large area of flat land.

plantation (plan-TAY-shuhn)
A large farm.

pluperfect tense (ploo-PER-fekt tens)
A tense that describes something that happened in the past before another action. Use *had + verb*. Example: Native Americans *had lived* in the Americas for centuries before the Europeans arrived.

pneumonia (nu-MOHN-yah)
A disease of the lungs, which makes people have difficulty breathing.

political map (po-LI-ti-kuhl map)
A map that shows countries, states, or regions. It also shows cities, towns, and capitals.

porcelain (POR-si-luhn)
A hard, shiny white material that is used to make plates, cups, etc.

possessive nouns (puh-ZE-siv nownz)
Nouns that end in an apostrophe (') *s* to show that something belongs to someone. Example: A lord's manor.

pottery (PAH-ter-ee)
Jars, jugs, and other items made out of clay.

predict (pree-DIKT)
A reading strategy where you guess what you will read about after previewing.

prefix (PREE-fiks)
A beginning added to a word that changes the meaning.

preview (PREE-vyoo)
A reading strategy where you look quickly at the headings, captions, and pictures in a text before reading it.

primary source (PREYE-mair-ee sors)
An original document that was written or made at the time events happened.

printing press (PRIN-ting pres)
A machine that prints newspapers, books, and other writing.

prison (PRI-zin)
A place where people who commit crimes are held for punishment.

pronoun (PROH-nown)
A word that replaces a noun. Example: Harriet Tubman was an abolitionist. *She* was an abolitionist.

prophet (PRAH-fit)
Someone who says what will happen in the future and teaches people about religion. Muhammad was believed to be a prophet.

protests (PROH-tests)
A strong public complaint about something that you disagree with or think is unfair.

pyramid (PEER-uh-mid)
A large structure made from stone blocks. The Egyptians, Mayas, and Aztecs all built pyramids.

racism (RAY-si-zuhm)
The belief that some races of people are better than others.

railroads (RAYL-rohdz)
The system of train tracks and other equipment.

Reformation (re-for-MAY-shuhn)
A movement started by Martin Luther in the 1500s to reform, or change, the Roman Catholic Church. The Reformation resulted in the creation of the Protestant Church.

region (REE-juhn)
A large area that shares at least one common feature.

Renaissance (REN-uh-sahns)
A period of cultural change that began in Italy in the late 1300s and spread all over Europe. During this time, an interest in classical ideas, art, and literature was reborn. The Renaissance lasted until the 1600s.

representatives (re-pri-ZEN-tuh-tivz)
People who are chosen to do something for someone else.

reread (ree-REED)
A reading strategy where you read the text again to help you to understand it better.

resources (REE-sor-siz)
Things such as land, oil, and minerals that a country has and can use to trade and get richer.

revolt (ri-VOHLT)
A strong and often violent action against the government.

revolution (re-vuh-LOO-shuhn)
A time of great, usually sudden, social and political change.

river (RI-ver)
A continuous flow of water that goes into the ocean or a lake.

route (root) or (rowt)
The way from one place to another, especially one that is shown on a map.

ruler (ROO-ler)
Somebody who has official power over a country and its people.

sarcophagus (sar-KAH-fah-guhs)
Another name for a *coffin*, in which a dead body is placed.

science (SEYE-yuhnts)
The study of the natural world.

sculptures (SKULP-cherz)
Artistic objects made from wood, stone, clay or metal.

sea (see)
A large area of salt water that is smaller than an ocean.

selective attention
(se-LEK-tiv uh-TEN-shuhn)
A reading strategy where you focus on the information that you need to remember in order to answer a question or write about a topic.

senate (SE-nuht)
A group of people in the government that makes laws and advises other parts of the government.

settlers (SET-lerz)
People who make a home, or settle, in a new place.

shogun (SHOH-guhn)
The leader of the most powerful samurai clan in Japan, the Minamoto clan. The shogun was a military leader and was given the power to rule Japan.

silk (silk)
A soft material made from a fiber produced by silkworms.

simple past tense (SIM-puhl past tens)
To form the simple past tense, add -ed or -d. Example: hunt → hunted; love → loved

Sirius (SEE-ree-uhs)
A bright star that helped the ancient Egyptians make a calendar.

slaves (slayvz)
People who belonged to someone else and worked for no pay.

social studies (SOH-shuhl STUH-deez)
The study of history, geography, economics, and government.

society (suh-SEYE-uh-tee)
A group of people who live in the same country and have the same customs.

south (sowth)
One of the four points on the compass rose.

southern (SUH-thern)
In or from the south part of something.

structure (STRUHK-cher)
Something that has been built.

submarine (suhb-muh-REEN)
A type of boat that can travel underwater.

suffix (SUH-fiks)
An ending added to a word that changes its meaning.

summarize (SUHM-uh-reyez)
A reading strategy where you take information and say it or write it in fewer words.

superlatives (soo-PER-luh-tivs)
Words used to show that something is the longest, biggest, or best when compared to other things. To form a superlative, take an adjective and add -est. Example: The Nile River is the longest river in the world.

Swahili (swah-HEE-lee)
The most widely spoken language in East Africa.

tax (taks)
Money added to something you buy, or subtracted from a paycheck, that goes to the government.

territory (TAIR-i-tor-ee)
Land owned by a government.

terrorism (TAIR-er-i-zuhm)
A violent political action by a person or a group of people.

timeline (teyem-leyen)
A timeline shows what happened over a long period of time.

tomb (toom)
A place where a sarcophagus, or coffin, is put.

trade (trayd)
The buying and selling of goods.

treaty (TREE-tee)
An official written agreement.

Treaty of Versailles (TREE-tee uhv ver-SEYE)
The treaty signed between the Allies and Germany in 1919 at the end of World War I.

tribe (treyeb)
A community of people with a common culture that live in one place.

tsunami (soo-NAH-mee)
A large ocean wave that is usually caused by an underwater earthquake or volcanic explosion. A tsunami can travel across an entire ocean. If a tsunami reaches land, it can cause great damage.

unemployment (uhn-em-PLOI-muhnt)
The condition of not having a job.

Union (YOON-yuhn)
The name for the northern states during the American Civil War.

united (yoo-NEYE-tuhd)
Joined together.

use what you know (yooz wuht yoo noh)
A reading strategy where you use what you already know about a topic to understand new information.

valley (VA-lee)
An area of lower land between rows of hills or mountains.

vassal (VA-suhl)
Someone in the feudal system who held land for his king or lord in exchange for protection.

visualize (VIZH-yoo-uh-leyez)
A reading strategy where you try to imagine what you are reading. When you visualize, you create a picture in your mind.

volcano (vuhl-KAY-noh)
A mountain with a hole in the middle that burning rock and fire can come out of.

voyage (VOI-yuhj)
A long trip, especially by boat or ship.

wagon train (WA-guhn trayn)
A group of covered wagons that travels together. Pioneers traveled westward in wagon trains.

weather (WE-ther)
The temperature and the state of the wind, rain, and sun.

west (west)
One of the four points on a compass rose.

western (WES-tern)
In or from the west part of something.

Understanding the Past Tense

Simple Past Tense of Regular Verbs

When you read social studies, you often read about things that have already happened. In English, we use the past tense to show that something has happened. When you learn to recognize the past tense, you can understand more of the reading.

Use the simple past tense to talk about events that started and finished in the past.

They worked. **Now**

Past ←——————————————————————————————→ **Future**

- Form the simple past tense of regular verbs by adding *-ed* or *-d* to the base form of the verb.

    World War II **ended** in 1945.
    end ——→ end**ed**

    We **sailed** on the ocean.
    sail ——→ sail**ed**

    They **lived** in houses.
    live ——→ liv**ed**

- Sometimes the spelling of words changes when you add *-ed*.

    Sacagawea **cried** out for help.
    cry ——→ cr**ied**

    They **stopped** in New Mexico.
    stop ——→ stop**ped**

- You can use the simple past tense to talk about a group of events that started and finished in the past.

    They **hunted** buffalo, **raised** corn, and **fished** in the rivers and lakes.

Practice

Form the simple past tense of the verb in parentheses. Write the sentences in your notebook.

Example: They _wanted_ (want) to find gold and silver.

1. They _____ (ask) the king for help.

2. The American Revolution _____ (start) in Massachusetts.

3. The men and women _____ (plant) rice.

4. The factory _____ (need) more workers.

5. She _____ (design) and _____ (sew) the new flag.

6. He _____ (learn) to read when he was twenty-one.

7. First it _____ (rain), then it _____ (hail), and finally it _____ (snow).

8. Many families _____ (move) from the farms to the cities.

9. The explorers _____ (discover) new routes.

10. He _____ (sign) the Constitution.

▲ They planted rice.

For more practice,
go to Workbook page 129.

Negative Statements About the Past

Form negative statements about the past by adding the word *didn't* in front of the base form of the verb. *Didn't* is the contraction of *did + not*.

They **didn't have** food for the winter.

He **didn't know** the answer.

The soldiers **didn't bring** good news.

Practice

Make each statement negative. Write the sentences in your notebook.

Example: The government taxed tea.
The government didn't tax tea.

1. They added an amendment.

   _____

2. He started a new political party.

   _____

3. They wanted to settle in the West.

   _____

4. It arrived on time.

   _____

5. She thanked them for their help.

   _____

6. They believed in many different gods.

   _____

7. The law ended slavery.

   _____

8. They developed a calendar.

   _____

9. They tried to grow a new kind of wheat.

   _____

10. I liked the way the story ended.

    _____

For more practice,
go to Workbook page 130.

Simple Past Tense of Irregular Verbs

Some verbs are irregular. They do not end in -*ed* in the simple past tense.

- Some irregular verbs change their vowels in the simple past tense.

    The soldier **ran** to the general.

    run ——→ **ran**

Here are some examples of irregular verbs that change their vowels in the simple past.

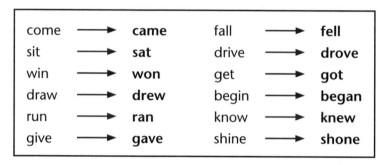

come	——→	**came**	fall ——→	**fell**
sit	——→	**sat**	drive ——→	**drove**
win	——→	**won**	get ——→	**got**
draw	——→	**drew**	begin ——→	**began**
run	——→	**ran**	know ——→	**knew**
give	——→	**gave**	shine ——→	**shone**

- Some irregular verbs stay the same in the past tense.

    He **hurt** his arm.

    hurt ——→ **hurt**

Here are some examples of verbs that stay the same in the simple past.

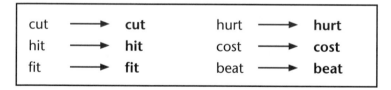

cut	——→	**cut**	hurt ——→	**hurt**
hit	——→	**hit**	cost ——→	**cost**
fit	——→	**fit**	beat ——→	**beat**

- In negative statements, add *didn't* before the base form of the verb.

    The soldier **didn't run** to the general.

    He **didn't hurt** his arm.

- Some verbs, like *be,* change completely in the simple past.

I **am**	I **was**
He/She/It **is**	He/She/It **was**
We/You/They **are**	We/You/They **were**

- Use the verb *be* to talk about the past. You can also use *be* to ask and answer questions about the past and to make statements about events that happened in the past.

  He **was** a soldier in the war.
  Was he a soldier in the war? Yes, he **was**.

  They **were** slaves.
  Were they slaves? Yes, they **were**.

- To make a negative statement with *be* in the past, use *wasn't* or *weren't*. *Wasn't* is the contraction of *was + not* and *weren't* is the contraction of *were + not*.

  Was he the first president of the United States?
  No, he **was not**.

  Were they happy to see her?
  No, they **were not**.

  Was he the vice president?
  No, he **wasn't**.

  Were there many people there?
  No, there **weren't**.

- You can also use the simple past tense of the verb *be* to ask *wh-* questions.

  Why **were** they there?

  Who **was** Benjamin Franklin?

Here are some other verbs that change completely in the simple past tense.

have	**had**	do	**did**	
go	**went**	see	**saw**	
fight	**fought**	write	**wrote**	
keep	**kept**	say	**said**	
tell	**told**	leave	**left**	
think	**thought**	find	**found**	
break	**broke**	lead	**led**	
take	**took**	stand	**stood**	
bring	**brought**	choose	**chose**	
teach	**taught**	buy	**bought**	

Practice

Form the simple past tense of the verb in parentheses. Write the sentences in your notebook.

Example: He ___*was*___ (be) the first governor of the state.

1. They _____ (write) the Bill of Rights.

2. He _____ (not find) a new continent.

3. Her grandfather _____ (fight) in World War II.

4. John F. Kennedy _____ (try) to end discrimination.

5. They _____ (not keep) the plans to themselves.

6. Sacagawea _____ (tell) Lewis and Clark where to go.

Rewrite each sentence as a *wh-* question.

Example: They tried to land on the moon.   (What?)
           What did they try to do?

1. They chose a name for the city.   (What?)

   _____

2. He brought a copy of the Constitution.   (What?)

   _____

3. They needed help because there was no food.   (Why?)

   _____

4. She wanted to live in the United States.   (Where?)

   _____

5. The stock market crashed in 1929.   (When?)

   _____

6. They wanted religious freedom.   (What?)

   _____

For more practice, go to Workbook pages 131–132.

The following paragraph is about César Chavez. Fill in each blank with the correct past tense of the verb in parentheses. Write the paragraph in your notebook.

The people in César Chavez's family ___were___ (be) migrant workers. They _____ (1. travel) all over California, picking different kinds of crops. Chavez _____ (2. see) that people _____ (3. pay) migrant workers very little for their work. The workers _____ (4. have) terrible working conditions. As an adult, Chavez _____ (5. want) to help agricultural workers get their rights. Chavez _____ (6. organize) nonviolent protests to convince employers to pay workers higher wages. He _____ (7. get) the idea for nonviolent actions from Martin Luther King Jr. and Mahatma Gandhi. Chavez _____ (8. teach) others to demand their rights peacefully. Thousands of migrant workers _____ (9. follow) Chavez's example. They _____ (10. help) improve conditions for today's workers.

▲ César Chavez

For more practice, go to Workbook pages 133–134.

Index

Credits

Kindersley; 100 right, Geoff Dann/Dorling Kindersley; 101, Royalty-Free/CORBIS; 102, Skjold Photographs; 103, DK Cartography; 104, Church of San Vitale, Ravenna, Italy/Canali PhotoBank, Milan/SuperStock; 105, Reuters/CORBIS; 106, Peter Visscher/Dorling Kindersley; 107 left, Scala/Art Resource, NY; 107 right, The Cleveland Museum of Art; 108 left, The Granger Collection, New York; 108 right, The Granger Collection, New York; 109, © The British Library/The Bridgeman Art Library; 110 left, Archivo Iconografico, S.A./CORBIS; 110 right, Royalty-Free/CORBIS; 111 left, Historical Picture Archive/CORBIS; 111 right, The Granger Collection, New York; 113, DK Cartography; 114 top right, Yoshitora/The Bridgeman Art Library; 114 bottom right, The National Palace Museum, Taipei, Taiwan, Republic of China; 114 top left, © The British Museum/Alan Hills/Dorling Kindersley; 114 bottom left, John Wang/Photodisc/Getty Images; 115, George H. H. Huey/CORBIS; 116, SW Productions/Photodisc/Getty Images; 117, DK Cartography; 118 left, DK Cartography; 118 right, Jeannette Williams/Omni-Photo Communications, Inc.; 119 left, © The British Library/Dorling Kindersley; 119 right, Cary Wolinsky/Aurora; 120, Art Resource, NY; 121, *Marco Polo with Kubilaj Khan in Peking, 1375*/Ms. 2810/Bibliotheque Nationale, Paris; 122 left, DK Cartography; 122 right, Andy Crawford/Dorling Kindersley; 123 left, Pearson Education U.S. ELT/Scott Foresman; 123 right, Corel Corporation; 124 left, Jack Stein Grove/PhotoEdit; 124 right, George Holton/Photo Researchers, Inc.; 125, Tony Linck/SuperStock; 127, DK Cartography; 129, DK Cartography; 131, Barnabas Kindersley/Dorling Kindersley.

UNIT 4 132–133, Philip Craven/Robert Harding World Imagery; 134 bottom, Peter Dennis/Dorling Kindersley; 134 top right, Dagli Orti/Museo Franz Mayer Mexico/The Art Archive; 134 top left, Dagli Orti/Marine Museum, Lisbon/The Art Archive; 135 left, Erich Lessing/Art Resource, NY; 135 middle, © The British Library; 135 right, Inc., Martin Paul Ltd./Index Stock Imagery; 136, Michael Newman/PhotoEdit; 137, DK Cartography; 138, Bettmann/CORBIS; 139 left, David Ashby/Dorling Kindersley; 139 right, Hulton Archive Photos/Getty Images; 140 left, DK Cartography; 140 right, Dorling Kindersley; 141 left, Denis Waugh/Allstock/Getty Images; 141 right, Michelangelo Buonarroti (Caprese 1475–Roma 1564), *The Libyan Sibyl*, Fresco, 1508–1512. Vatican Palace, Sistine Chapel; 142, *La Gioconda, (Mona Lisa)*/Leonardo da Vinci (1452–1519)/Musée du Louvre, Paris, France/oil on wood, 30 1/4" x 21" (76.8 x 53.5 cm)/Lewandowski/LeMage/Art Resource, NY; 143 top left, Bettmann/CORBIS; 143 bottom left, Pearson Learning Photo Studio/Pearson Learning; 143 top right, Matthew Ward/Dorling Kindersley; 144, Granger/The Granger Collection, New York; 145 left, DK Cartography; 145 right, SuperStock; 147, DK Cartography; 148 top left, The Granger Collection, New York; 148 top right, Courtesy of The National Maritime Museum, London/James Stevenson/Dorling Kindersley; 148 bottom, Sallie Alane Reason/Dorling Kindersley; 148 middle, Diego Duran/The Bridgeman Art Library/Biblioteca Nacional, Madrid; 149,

Bernardino de Sahagun/The Granger Collection, New York; 150, Leonardo da Vinci/The Granger Collection, New York; 151 top, DK Cartography; 151 bottom, DK Cartography; 152 left, Dagli Orti/Marine Museum, Lisbon/The Art Archive; 152 right, Myrleen Ferguson Cate/PhotoEdit; 153 left, © 1996 North Wind Pictures; 153 right, Bibliotheque Nationale, Paris/Giraudon/Art Resource, NY; 154 left, Dagli Orti/Museo de la Torre del Oro, Seville/The Art Archive; 154 right, Bernardino de Sahagun/The Granger Collection, New York; 155, Peter Dennis/Dorling Kindersley; 156, Charles & Josette Lenars/CORBIS; 157 left, Charles & Josette Lenars/CORBIS; 157 top right, Bettmann/CORBIS; 157 bottom right, Museo Nacional de Arqueologia, Antropologia E Historia del Peru; 158 bottom, Bettmann/CORBIS; 158 top, Art Resource, NY; 159 left, Private Collection/The Bridgeman Art Library; 159 right, Courtesy of the London Dungeon/Alex Wilson/Dorling Kindersley; 161 left, DK Cartography; 161 right, DK Cartography; 163, DK Cartography; 165, Leonardo da Vinci/Edimédia/CORBIS.

UNIT 5 166–167, Adolf Pannash/Courtesy of Schwenkfelder Library & Heritage Center, Pennsburg, PA; 168 top right, Hulton Archive Photos/Getty Images; 168 top left, The Granger Collection, New York; 168 bottom, SuperStock; 169, The Granger Collection, New York; 170, Jay Penni/Prentice Hall School Division; 172 bottom, David Ashby/Dorling Kindersley; 172 top, The National Maritime Museum, London/Tina Chambers/Dorling Kindersley; 173, Bettmann/CORBIS; 174 left, Bettmann/CORBIS; 174 right, The New York Public Library/Art Resource, NY; 175 left, Hulton Archive Photos/Getty Images; 175 top right, Hulton Archive Photos/Getty Images; 175 bottom right, Bettmann/CORBIS; 176 left, *The Mayflower in Plymouth Harbor*/William Formsby Halsall/Burstein Collection/CORBIS; 176 right, Michael Littlejohn/Pearson Education/Prentice Hall College; 177, Hulton Archive Photos/Getty Images; 178, *Portrait of a Negro Man, Olaudah Equiano*/Royal Albert Memorial Museum, Exeter, Devon, U.K./1780s, (previously attributed to Joshua Reynolds) by English School (18th century)/The Bridgeman Art Library; 179 left, J. W. Orr/The Library of Congress; 179 right, © Judith Miller/Freeman's/Dorling Kindersley; 181 middle left, Cary Wolinsky/Aurora; 181 left, Cary Wolinsky/Aurora; 181 middle right, Cary Wolinsky/Aurora; 181 right, Cary Wolinsky/Aurora; 182 top left, Hulton Archive Photos/Getty Images; 182 right, Hulton Archive Photos/Getty Images; 182 bottom, *The Boston Tea Party*, 16 December 1773, colored engraving, 19th century/The Granger Collection, New York; 183, CORBIS; 186, The *Bostonians Paying the Excise-Man* or *Tarring & Feathering*/Philip Dawe (c. 1750–c.1785)/colored engraving/The Gilder Lehman Collection on deposit at The Pierpont Morgan Library, London, 1774/GL 4961.01/Photography: Joseph Zehavi/Art Resource, NY; 187 left, Hulton Archive Photos/Getty Images; 187 right, Getty Images; 188, The Granger Collection, New York; 189 left, Alonzo Chappel/Bettmann/CORBIS; 189 middle, Dorling Kindersley; 189 right, Courtesy of the

95th Rifles and Re-enactment Living History Unit/Geoff Brightling/Dorling Kindersley; 190 bottom, *The Declaration of Independence, 4 July 1776*/John Trumbull (American, 1756–1843)/1786–1820/oil on canvas/53 x 78.7 cm. (20 7/8 x 31 in.)/Bettmann/CORBIS; 190 top, *Thomas Jefferson* (1743-1826) by Rembrandt Peale, c. 1805, detail, oil on canvas, 28 x 23 1/2", Collection of The New-York Historical Society; 191 left, *The Surrender of Lord Cornwallis at Yorktown, 19 October 1781*/John Trumbull (American 1756–1843)/1787–c. 1828/oil on canvas, 53.3 x 77.8 x 1.9 cm. (21 x 30 5/8 x 3/4 in.)/Trumbull Collection/Yale University Art Gallery; 191 right, Terry Vine/Allstock/Getty Images; 192, Hulton Archive Photos/Getty Images; 193 left, *George Washington* (Vaughan portrait), Gilbert Stuart, 1795, oil on canvas. 29" x 23 3/4"/Andrew W. Mellon Collection/© Board of Trustees/The National Gallery of Art, Washington, D.C.; 193 right, Alfred Pasieka/Peter Arnold, Inc.; 195, chart adapted from *Land, People, Nation: A History of the United States, Beginnings to 1977* by Anna Uhl Chamot and Kathleen Anderson Steeves, 2nd edition/© Pearson Education, Inc. Reprinted by permission of Pearson Education, Inc., Upper Saddle River, NJ.; 199, SW Productions/Photodisc/Getty Images.

UNIT 6 200–201, Currier & Ives/The Granger Collection, New York; 202 right, © California State Library Foundation/ Courtesy of the California History Room/California State Library, Sacramento, California; 202 bottom left, Western History Collection/The Denver Public Library; 202 top left, © Gilcrease Museum, Tulsa; 202 middle left, Bettmann/ CORBIS; 203, Smithsonian Institution/Office of Imaging, Printing, and Photographic Services; 206 left, Todd Gipstein/CORBIS; 206 right, The Granger Collection, New York; 207 left, Hulton Archive Photos/Getty Images; 207 right, American Numismatic Society of New York; 208, Photodisc/Getty Images; 209 left, The Granger Collection, New York; 209, right, Bettmann/CORBIS; 210 left, William Henry Jackson/The Granger Collection, New York; 210 right, Pearson Learning Photo Studio/Pearson Learning; 211 left, *Ahead of the Storm*, Tim Cox, 1989, oil, 12" x 16"/ Courtesy of Eagle Creek Enterprises; 211 right, Reuters/ CORBIS; 212, The Granger Collection, New York; 213 left, John Woodcock/Dorling Kindersley; 213 right, Keith Wood/Allstock/Getty Images; 216 bottom, Vladimir Kordic/ National Geographic Image Collection; 216 middle, Hulton Archive Photos/Getty Images; 216 top, The Granger Collection, New York; 217, Frances F. Palmer/Museum of the City of New York/CORBIS; 219, Historical Statistics of the United States; 220 left, The Granger Collection, New York; 220 right, Hulton Archive Photos/Getty Images; 221 left, United States Signal Corps; 221 right, Hulton Archive Photos/Getty Images; 222 left, The Library of Congress; 222 right, UPI/Bettmann/CORBIS; 223 left, Hulton Archive Photos/Getty Images; 223 right, Bureau of Indian Affairs/U.S. Department of the Interior; 224, Christie's Images/CORBIS; 225, Frederic Remington/Hulton Archive Photos/Getty Images; 226 left, *The Biermeister & Main Steel Forge*/Peter Severin Kroyer (1851–1909)/Statens Museum for Kunst, Copenhagen, Denmark/The Bridgeman Art Library, London/SuperStock; 226 right, Charmet, J-L/ Photo Researchers, Inc.; 227 left, Dr. Jeremy Burgess/ Photo Researchers, Inc.; 227 middle left, Con Edison of New York; 227 middle right, CORBIS; 227 right, Ford Motor Company; 229 top, Historical Statistics of the United States; 229 right, Dorling Kindersley; 231, graphs from *Land, People, Nation: A History of the United States, Beginnings to 1977* by Anna Uhl Chamot and Kathleen Anderson Steeves, 2nd edition/© Pearson Education, Inc./ Reprinted by permission of Pearson Education, Inc., Upper Saddle River, NJ.; 233, Seth Eastman/Geoffrey Clements/CORBIS.

UNIT 7 234 left, *Louisville Flood Victims*/Margaret Bourke-White, 1937/Life magazine/Time & Life Pictures/Getty Images; 234–235 top, Benelux Press/Index Stock Imagery; 234–235 middle, © John Berry/The Image Works; 234–235 right, Underwood & Underwood/CORBIS; 234–235 bottom, Thomas Kienzzle/AP/Wide World Photos; 236 top left, Bettmann/CORBIS; 236 bottom left, Hulton-Deutsch Collection/CORBIS; 236 top right, Hulton-Deutsch Collection/CORBIS; 236 middle right, UPI/CORBIS; 236 bottom right, CORBIS; 237, Bettmann/CORBIS; 239 top, Myrleen Ferguson/PhotoEdit; 239 middle left, Pearson Longman ELT; 239 middle right, Silver Burdett Ginn; 239 bottom, David K. Crow/PhotoEdit; 240 left, The Library of Congress; 240 right, Tobi Zausner; 241, Hulton Archive Photos/Getty Images; 242 left, DK Cartography; 242 top right, Bettmann/CORBIS; bottom right, Vivian Dalziel Bernard (soldier)/© Virginia Bernard; 243 left, Bettmann/CORBIS; 243 right, Andrea Brizzi/Stock Market/CORBIS; 244 left, Brown Brothers; 244 right, AP/Wide World Photos; 245 left, DK Cartography; 245 right, National Archives and Records Administration; 246, SuperStock; 247 left, Max Desfor/AP/Wide World Photos; 247 right, U.S. Air Force; 249, DK Cartography; 250 top left, Dario Lopez-Mills/AP/Wide World Photos; 250 bottom left, Minosa/Scorpio/Sygma/CORBIS; 250 right, Maria Voron/The Granger Collection, New York; 251, AEF/Serge Attal/Image Bank/Getty Images; 252, Hulton Archive Photos/Getty Images; 253 top left, Dorling Kindersley; 253 top right, David Young-Wolff/PhotoEdit; 253 bottom, John A. Rizzo/Photodisc/Getty Images; 254 bottom, Map Resources/Adaptation by Wendy Wolf; 254 right, UPI/CORBIS; 255 left, Bettmann/CORBIS; 255 right, AP/Wide World Photos; 256 bottom, The Library of Congress; 256 top, NASA; 257, Peter Turnley/CORBIS; 258 left, Bettmann/CORBIS; 258 right, Colin Walton/Dorling Kindersley; 259 left, Jeff Widener/AP/Wide World Photos; 259 right, Mike Yamashita/Woodfin Camp & Associates; 260 left, Frank Kroenke/Peter Arnold, Inc.; 260 right, Peter Turnley/CORBIS; 261, © Wesley Bocxe/The Image Works; 263, John A. Rizzo/Photodisc/Getty Images.

BACK MATTER 280, Demetrio Carrasco/Dorling Kindersley; 285, National Archives and Records Administration.